More Praise for *Mastering the Addicted Brain*

"The disease of addiction is killing more people than any other nonnatural cause — more than guns and car accidents combined. At a time when we're losing so many of our loved ones, Walter Ling's *Mastering the Addicted Brain* is a revelation. Dr. Ling, one of the world's foremost experts on addiction, explains addiction in a way that non-scientists can understand, and he dispels the pervasive myth that this disease can't be treated. Indeed, over the course of his decades-long career, Dr. Ling has shown not only that people with addiction can get well but also *how* they can. If you or a loved one is suffering addiction — or if you want to understand a disease that's devastating our families, communities, and nation — this book is indispensable. It's a guide to changing lives — and saving them."

— **David Sheff,** author of *Beautiful Boy: A Father's Journey through His Son's Addiction* and *Clean: Overcoming Addiction and Ending America's Greatest Tragedy*

"Dr. Walter Ling is the nation's foremost expert in the use of medications to treat addiction, which explains his nuanced understanding of the limited role that medications play in treating the addicted brain, and his emphasis on the importance of building a sane and meaningful life to obtain and maintain recovery. In this deceptively simple book, Dr. Ling reminds the reader that stopping drug and alcohol use is only the first, and perhaps easiest, step in treating addiction, with the hard work beginning as a new life unfolds."

— **... on, RN, PhD, FAAN,** Associate ... ineringen Endowed Chair, Department of Family and Community Health, University of Pennsylvania School of Nursing

"This beautifully written book by a prominent figure in addiction medicine provides a useful perspective for individuals whose pleasure-seeking, feel-better use of opiates has led to addiction. The book could also have been titled *Getting to Know Walter Ling: Neurologist, Psychiatrist, Practitioner, Philosopher, Family Man*. His wit and wisdom contribute to the appeal of his message for an even wider audience of interested readers."
— **C. James Klett, PhD**

"*Mastering the Addicted Brain* is an engaging, informative, and evidence-based treatise on drug addiction. It offers a nonjudgmental perspective on how people become addicted and how to cope with the addiction after it happens. Like Dr. Ling himself, the book is filled with compassion, wisdom, and funny stories. Most of all, it provides a road map for how to lead a happy, balanced, and meaningful life. Addicts, their friends and family, and anyone who has struggled with difficult problems will benefit from reading this book."
— **Sandra D. Comer, PhD,** Professor of Neurobiology, Department of Psychiatry, Columbia University and New York State Psychiatric Institute

"There are many scientific journals about the neuroscience of addiction. There are also lots of popular books written about recovery for the general public. There are very few entertaining and easy-to-read books about addiction that are scientifically accurate and also contain gems of ancient wisdom. Dr. Ling has provided the latter in this wonderful little handbook that contains all the essentials of recovery and a wonderful first chapter for everyone who has ever known someone struggling with this most difficult disease."
— **Jeanne L. Obert, MFT, MSM,** cofounder and board chair, Matrix Institute on Addictions

"An amazing amount of information is packed into this very readable little book. Walter Ling is one of the pioneers in the field of addiction, and anyone who is affected by addiction can learn from the wisdom of this master."

— **Richard A. Rawson, PhD,** Research Professor, Vermont Center on Behavior and Health

"*Mastering the Addicted Brain* is the perfect guide to support clinicians. It provides practical, evidence-based guidance along with an easy-to-understand conceptualization of how addiction occurs. It's useful for those who have an addiction as well as the family and friends of those who need support in their recovery. Highly recommended."

— **Robert Ali,** Associate Professor of Pharmacology, University of Adelaide School of Medicine

"Over the past forty years, Dr. Walter Ling and his colleagues have contributed more than any other group of clinical scientists to more-effective treatments for all addictions. With this short, easy-to-read summary of his research findings and clinical wisdom, Dr. Ling has opened the door for clinicians, educators, and affected families to understand and ultimately 'master' addiction. There are not yet cures for addictions, but this book shows how it is possible — indeed expectable — to overcome drug cravings and relapses and to develop a rewarding life in recovery."

— **A.Thomas McLellan,** addiction researcher and founder of Treatment Research Institute

"This book is delightful and easy to read, yet conveys a profound understanding of what addiction is and what it takes to overcome addiction. It is full of useful insights, thoughtful exercises, and sound advice to guide individuals along the difficult road to recovery. This book will be helpful to patients and their families as well as professionals in the addiction field."

— **Kathleen Brady, MD, PhD,** former president,
American Academy of Addiction Psychiatry

"Dr. Walter Ling's *Mastering the Addicted Brain* makes the very complicated and complex information on the disease of addiction simple and direct. He explains with profound clarity the difference between getting addicted and staying addicted and getting sober and staying sober. As an addiction expert for the past twenty-two years, I've found that these concepts are the most common challenges for my clients and their families to understand, accept, and heal. In well-laid-out steps and exercises, Dr. Ling offers guidance, support, and a simple plan for long-term recovery."

— **Kristina Wandzilak, CAS, CIP,** author of
The Lost Years: Surviving a Mother and Daughter's Worst Nightmare and founder of Full Circle Intervention and Full Circle Addiction and Recovery Services

"Walter Ling is an addiction physician and researcher with several decades of experience as well as extensive knowledge on which to draw. Nevertheless, the book remains highly accessible and understandable to a wide readership, including those with no prior medical or scientific understanding of addictions, the associated harms, or the processes whereby addictions can be mastered. This is a very valuable book for those afflicted by addictions, for their family and friends, and for the interested general public."

— **Professor Sir John Strang,**
National Addiction Centre, King's College London

Mastering *the* Addicted Brain

Mastering *the* Addicted Brain

*Building a Sane and
Meaningful Life to Stay Clean*

~

WALTER LING, MD

FOREWORD BY ALAN I. LESHNER, PhD

New World Library
Novato, California

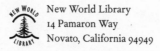

New World Library
14 Pamaron Way
Novato, California 94949

Text design by Tona Pearce Myers

Library of Congress Cataloging-in-Publication Data
Names: Ling, Walter, author.
Title: Mastering the addicted brain : building a sane and meaningful life to stay clean / Walter Ling, M.D.
Description: Novato, California : New World Library, [2017] | Includes index.
  Identifiers: LCCN 2017026621 (print) | LCCN 2017027042 (ebook) | ISBN 9781608685011 (Ebook) | ISBN 9781608685004 (alk. paper)
Subjects: LCSH: Substance abuse—Treatment—Popular works. | Brain—Popular works.
Classification: LCC RC564 (ebook) | LCC RC564 .L496 2017 (print) | DDC 362.29—dc23
LC record available at https://lccn.loc.gov/2017026621

First printing, August 2017
Print ISBN 978-1-60868-500-4
Ebook ISBN 978-1-60868-501-1

Printed in Canada on 100% postconsumer-waste recycled paper

New World Library is proud to be a Gold Certified Environmentally Responsible Publisher. Publisher certification awarded by Green Press Initiative. www.greenpressinitiative.org

10   9   8   7   6   5

Contents

Foreword

~

In *Mastering the Addicted Brain*, Walter Ling has provided an easy-to-read, dual-purpose book in layperson's language. It offers a relatively simple but highly accurate summary of what modern science is showing about the nature of addiction and what to do about it. It also provides some very practical suggestions about ways to, as he puts it, "build a sane and meaningful life to stay clean."

Dr. Ling draws on over thirty years of basic and clinical scientific research to explain that we now know that addiction is a brain disease — a brain disease with behavioral components that is expressed in important social contexts, but a brain disease nonetheless. That fact has great significance because, in addition to suggesting treatment approaches, it helps explain why an addicted person can't "just say no to drugs." The brain disease concept, which has been gaining more and more recognition in both professional and lay-public settings, has taken some twenty years to gain broad acceptance. Among other implications, it dictates that public policy must go beyond relatively simple criminal-justice approaches to include public-health strategies of prevention and treatment. Dr. Ling also explains that addiction is a chronic, relapsing brain disease that is unique among chronic diseases. Among other qualities, its management is extremely complex, in large part because of its multiple interacting components — biological, behavioral, and social.

Along the way, Dr. Ling very clearly busts a variety of myths about addiction and its treatment. One of the most important clarifications is his explanation that taking anti-addiction medications is quite different from taking drugs. Another myth is that one needs to "want treatment" or "reach bottom" before treatment can be effective. Involuntary or mandated treatment can often be as effective as voluntary treatment episodes.

When he turns to advice on preventing relapse after successful treatment and how to build a fulfilling life in spite of one's addictions, Dr. Ling draws not only on scientific research but also on some of the more interesting and relevant ancient Chinese and Thai philosophical sayings, as well as some wisdom derived from his own mother. I think that many of us — whether professionals, patients, or family members — can resonate with his advice. There are many lessons for all of us in this delightful book.

— Alan I. Leshner, PhD,
Chief Executive Officer Emeritus of the
American Association for the Advancement of Science
and Former Director of the National Institute on Drug Abuse,
National Institutes of Health

Preface

Welcome!

This book is about getting off and staying off drugs and living a sane, meaningful drug-free life. It is written for people with drug addictions — particularly to opioids like heroin and prescription pain pills and stimulants like methamphetamine and cocaine — but the principles and suggestions can apply to overcoming any addiction, such as to alcohol, tobacco, food, and so on. The book combines the story of the treacherous, sometimes deadly journey of addiction with a step-by-step guide to getting out alive and starting over on the road to a full and satisfying life.

Whether you are reading this book for yourself or for someone you love or someone you know, whether you are a healthcare professional or are simply curious about addiction and the brain and how people get into and out of trouble, I hope you find the information relevant and useful. If you are dealing with addiction yourself, the book offers helpful suggestions throughout that are easy to understand and follow. However, consult with your doctor or counselor for guidance about applying these principles and ideas to your specific circumstances.

This book gathers and revises a variety of material that has been created over the years by my colleagues and myself to help our patients, their families, our counselors, and our trainees. I am pleased to say that many of us are still active and still work together. In addition to colleagues and friends, I have also borrowed freely from earlier pioneers in the field, including Alan Beck, Herb Kleber, Jim Klett, Alan Leshner, Alan Marlatt, Tom McLellan, Bill Miller, Chuck O'Brien, and others. Virtually no idea in this book is new, and whenever possible I try to give credit to the right person or source. In addition, over time, certain ideas can become distilled into common sayings, proverbs, fables, and so on. These evocative sayings have no "author," but they capture "commonsense" advice and practical wisdom in memorable ways. I was raised on such sayings, since my mother was very fond of them, and I've sprinkled some of her favorites throughout this book.

You might wonder, why does this book's title promise "mastering" addiction, rather than "getting rid of" addiction? That's because addiction permanently changes your brain. Once someone becomes an addict, they can learn to stop taking drugs, but afterward they will always have an addicted brain. Once your brain becomes addicted, it can always lead you back to an addicted life, since your brain decides how you will act, and being an addict means acting like an addict. Your brain is still you; it's just a changed you. You can learn to master your addicted brain and overcome the behavioral manifestations of addiction, but you can't really get rid of addiction without getting rid of yourself. And that wouldn't do you any good.

This book is designed to be short and easy to read. From beginning to end, it comes to around 31,000 words. At the normal reading rate of 250 words a minute, it can be completed in about two to three hours. One reason for the book's brevity is my dislike for long sermons and drawn-out Sunday school lessons. The book's principles can be stated simply, even when their application may take time and involve effort.

Just as importantly, I don't like including things that don't help do the job. You won't find any accusing, blaming, moralizing, guilt-tripping, or name-calling about addicts or addiction. These things just don't help, and they are demoralizing to the person in recovery seeking to change addictive behavior. This book doesn't judge or try to convince people to change. It offers practical advice for those ready to change.

That said, don't rush through the book, either. Take your time. Consider the best ways to apply the ideas and proposals to your personal circumstances or your specific life. The book includes regular "pauses" that remind you to do just that.

In the end, how much you get out of reading this book will depend on how much you put into it. Not in terms of money, but with your time and energy. As the saying goes, you get what you pay for. Invest in yourself, and I daresay it will be well worth the price.

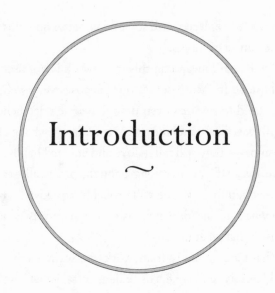

Introduction

∼

This book begins by discussing the brain, how it evolved to work the way it does, and how addiction is a brain disease. A person may not need this explanation to stop using drugs, but I think it helps to understand the framework I work from.

The idea that addiction is a brain disease is only a framework. While I consider it the best framework we have based on the latest scientific evidence, there are other ways to understand addiction. Further, this framework that addiction is a brain disease will probably be revised or even completely discarded one day. Like all other human theories, this one will at some point be proven incomplete, and then it will be replaced with something better and closer to the true nature of things.

That doesn't mean that this framework is not useful to us right now. In fact, it serves our purposes very well. My mother used to say that even though people once believed the earth was flat — and they were completely wrong about the cosmos — they still fell in love and enjoyed happy, productive lives. If you live long enough, practically everything that you think is true will probably be proved wrong, but so what? If our ideas help us to lead happy, productive lives, isn't that what matters?

What I am saying is, frameworks are scaffolds that help us build our lives; they help us achieve certain goals. As long as they are productive and useful, we should keep them. Once they stop being useful, we should change them. If you don't entirely agree with this book's framework, that's okay, but don't get too hung up on it and waste time arguing with it or agonizing over it. Test the strategies this book offers; keep those that help solve your problems, and discard the rest. This is why I don't dwell on frameworks that pin addiction to guilt and shame and sin and evil and weakness of will. In my experience, these frameworks don't help.

The key message in chapter 1 is that by understanding addiction as a brain disease, we can learn to deal with what really happens and exercise mastery over our behavior, while avoiding all the other baggage that saps our energy yet doesn't help solve the problem. In particular, I differentiate between becoming addicted and being addicted. They are not the same thing.

By the same token, getting off drugs is different from staying off drugs. As I discuss in chapter 2, "overcoming addiction" is defined by staying off drugs. Getting off drugs, or detoxification, is the necessary first step, but the foundation of a drug-free life is staying off drugs, or relapse prevention. Detoxification may be difficult, but relapse prevention is a life's work. Relapses do not happen by accident. They are the result of specific attitudes and actions. The bulk of this book, chapters 3 through 9, describes what to do to prevent relapse from happening.

If you struggle with addiction, you will discover that becoming drug-free does not get your old self back, which, even if you could do it, would not be enough to keep you off drugs. Remember, your old self got you into this mess to begin with. However, staying drug-free does get you back to "square one," as chapter 3 describes. From this place, you can make a new beginning and go in a new direction that will lead to a sane and meaningful life. And isn't that the real purpose of getting off and staying off drugs? Building a satisfying new life goes hand in hand with overcoming addiction.

That new life begins with, and depends on, getting into shape, both physically and mentally. As chapters 4 and 5 describe, it takes physical energy and sound emotional health to build a satisfying and meaningful life. That may sound mundane, but it is the foundation of overcoming addiction. If "square one" is a construction site, physical and mental health are your life's cement and steel. They're nothing pretty, but nothing strong, useful, or beautiful can be built without them. If the advice and practices in these chapters ever seem like a slog, be patient. Building good habits may seem tedious at times, that is, until the rewards manifest. Addicts who began using drugs as youth rarely learn this firsthand. For those addicts, it's fair to say they grew old but didn't grow up. Now is the time to grow up.

Growing up means taking care of yourself, but it also means taking care of and acting responsibly toward others, which chapters 6, 7, and 8 discuss. To stay off drugs, you have to do more than adopt a healthy lifestyle. You have to learn to take care of your own business as well as be a contributing member of your community — taking personal responsibility, making connections, developing trustworthiness, learning to love and be loved, being considerate of others, making friends, and being a friend. This is the true reward for a drug-free life: becoming a loved, necessary, and contributing member of one's community.

Finally, throughout the book I have included two types of special text: key phrases and "pauses." The key phrases, which appear in circles in the margins, simply highlight important points to remember, while "pauses" are reminders not to rush through the material. The pauses ask questions to encourage you to evaluate the book's ideas and consider how they might apply to your life. These pauses are like highway signs that announce "scenic view ahead." Pull over and contemplate the landscape and the horizon. Do you see a place you'd like to reach? Can you envision the road to get there? Take a mental picture to remember. When you come to a pause, take a break from reading and let what you are learning sink in so it will stay with you.

As I say, much of the advice in this book is common sense. You might think of it as the neuroscience of common sense. But still, you might wonder, and rightly so, will it work for me? Here's how you can tell if you are doing the right thing, and this applies to any addiction program you might be attending, such as Alcoholics Anonymous: If following the program, or attending the sessions, makes you feel like using, quit going. This is a sign you are heading in the wrong direction. But if the program makes you feel like staying off drugs and striving to be a better person, keep going.

Eventually, after you have achieved a certain degree of success and balance in your new, drug-free life, you will start to reflect on who you are and what you are here for. You will ponder and seek a meaningful life. You will reflect on what makes you happy being who you are, which raises the central question about addiction: Why do people take drugs to begin with? Why did you?

As we'll explore, people take drugs to feel good or to feel better; people take drugs in pursuit of happiness. But there are actually two kinds of happiness: One type focuses on personal pleasure, or having a good time for good time's sake, and the other type focuses on satisfaction, a uniquely human experience that arises when we feel good from doing good, when we are pleased with who we are. Pursuing only pleasure, ironically, harms our health and life, while pursuing satisfaction is always positive, since our happiness comes from giving happiness to others.

As the old saying goes, after all is said and done, there is always more said than done. A great deal has been said above, but we have only just begun. So let's get started. And remember, if this story of the journey makes sense to you, keep reading and practice the suggestions. Only action makes a difference.

Good luck and good learning.

CHAPTER ONE

Addiction Is a Brain Disease

How the Brain Gets and Stays Addicted

Hardly a day goes by without some researcher, politician, or policymaker saying that, based on forty years of scientific research, addiction should be considered a chronic brain disease and treated like any other chronic disease. Patients should have more ready access to treatment, in line with what's offered for chronic illnesses like heart disease. While that is all well and good, is it true that brain disease is the same as other chronic diseases? What does having a brain disease really mean for people suffering from addiction, for their families and friends, and for their physicians? This is both a medical and a philosophical question, or to put it more accurately, this is where medicine and philosophy come together.

The Framework of Brain Disease

Nearly two thousand years ago, the Greek physician and philosopher Galen observed that people with brain disease behave differently than those suffering from diseases of other body organs. He saw that when disease affects the brain, not just one certain body part stops working properly, but the whole person is affected. While a diseased body organ can make you very sick, people still recognize you as the person you are. Brain disease, however, affects the whole person — your sense of being a person, your personality, and your personhood. You are no longer the person you once were, and you are not the person your family and your friends once knew. People don't recognize who the addicted person has become, and sometimes addicts don't even recognize themselves.

When leaders and policymakers say we should treat addiction the way we treat hypertension, diabetes, and heart diseases, they are mainly arguing that doctors should treat addicted patients in the same way as patients with other chronic diseases, and health insurance should provide similar coverage. As a matter of policy, this is fine. However, it misses the mark to regard diseases of addiction as similar to other diseases. Brain disease affects much more than the body. Our brains define us in symbolic, metaphysical, moral, and spiritual ways. The brain is the organ of relationships, and its disease affects our relationship with our family, society, and God, not to mention ourselves. It is what makes us who we are.

That is why I want to explain what drugs do to the

brain, what happens to the brain on its way to becoming addicted and staying addicted, why people cannot just stop taking drugs when they want to, and why people take drugs to begin with. I want you to fully appreciate addiction as a brain disease.

That said, please remember that describing addiction as a "disease of the brain" is only a framework. A framework is not necessarily perfect or 100 percent accurate, and it doesn't have to be. We use frameworks to help us solve a problem in the most effective way, and I believe this framework for addiction does that. In time, as we understand addiction better, we may modify or even replace this framework, but only because a new framework works better at healing addiction.

Frameworks are most useful when they avoid any unnecessary, detrimental, or burdensome "baggage." Right now, the treatment of addiction is most often weighed down by the baggage of sin, blame, and faultfinding. While scientists describe and study addiction as a brain disease, as a society, which includes the medical profession, we still often treat people who suffer addiction as if they have sinned. But I believe we don't have to invoke guilt, shame, sin, or weakness of will in order to understand what happens in the brain or to treat drug addiction.

Say Hello to Your Brain

Let us begin by meeting our brain, or more accurately, our brains. Very simply, our brain is made up of three parts, which are really almost like three separate brains. The good news is that these three brains provide us with a good margin of safety in capacity, flexibility, and speed of thought. The bad news is that we have to keep the three brains running in harmony to work well, and most of the time the brains operate on their own, without our control or even awareness. We say we have an "integrated" brain when things run smoothly, but a lot can go wrong in a system like this — whether in one of the three brains or in the way they work together. But let's not get too far ahead of ourselves.

The first, oldest, and innermost of the three brains is our "reptilian" brain. This brain evolved along with the first lizards and crocodiles perhaps as long as three hundred million years ago. This primitive brain focuses on survival and has four basic functions: feeding, fighting, fleeing, and reproducing. Today, for us to have a smooth-running brain system, our main challenge is to let this survival brain do its job keeping us alive without dominating the other two brains, which arose later. Human lives are more complicated than those of crocs and lizards, and our reptilian brain needs to be kept under control.

Our second brain, the limbic brain, developed many millions of years later, along with the first mammals. The limbic brain focuses on memory and emotion. Its main job is to help us make connections and to keep us connected. It helps us bond and make lasting, meaningful relationships based on trust and love; it is the source of our happiness and our miseries. This brain determines our mood, whether we feel tough and cold or warm and fuzzy. Social mammals need emotion and memory; empathy and compassion, for ourselves and others, are necessary foundations of society, which requires individuals to balance self-interest against the welfare of others and the community. As we all know, this is not easy, but we use the limbic brain to negotiate this difficult terrain. And again, our main job is to let the limbic brain do its job without letting it get out of hand. Most emotional and behavioral problems, including addiction, have their roots in the limbic brain and its connections to — or the balance of power between it and — the reptilian brain and the cortical brain, which is our third brain.

The largest and most recent arrival, our cortical brain, is our thinking and decision-making brain. This makes us who we are as a species and as individuals. We depend on the cortical brain for our intelligence, our intuition, our creativity, and our appreciation of art and music and all things beautiful. It is the chief executive officer of our three-brain system. In many respects our cortical brain is still under construction; we are not sure where it will take us, but it is not an exaggeration to say that the survival of our human race depends on it. So far it has produced the fantastic scientific and technological innovations that have given us the comforts of modern life, but it has also given us the capacity to destroy ourselves and this planet we call home.

The harmonious working of our three-part brain gives rise to something more than the sum of its parts: a sense of self-awareness. Our minds are capable of observing our own thoughts, so that we can consciously direct, exercise, and improve ourselves. This sense of self — of self-consciousness — makes it possible to wonder about and search for the meaning of life, such as when we ask, "Who am I? Why am I here? What is the meaning of all this?" However, the exact relationship between our self-aware mind and our physical brain is unclear. Although the mind needs the brain in order to express itself, that doesn't mean the mind is the product of the brain. A good analogy is TV: The programs we watch are not produced by the television set, although we need the set to view them. Where the mind comes from and where it resides remains one big mystery.

In any case, using this greatly simplified model of our brain, we can discuss the disease of addiction. Many things can go wrong with each of our three brains individually, but more often the problem is that one brain has too much or too little power relative to the others.

How the Brain Becomes Addicted

At the simplest physical level, the brain functions using a combination of electricity and chemistry. Electric circuits give the brain its speed, but at the cellular level, the brain works chemically. It is one big chemical machine.

In the story of addiction, the main protagonist — usually a hero, but here a villain — is the chemical dopamine. Dopamine is the motivational or "feel-good" chemical, which is released in our limbic brain by such rewarding experiences as food, sex, and drugs. Dopamine also helps release the "cuddling" hormone oxytocin, which makes us want to repeat these experiences. Different levels of dopamine are released by different stimuli. For instance, during an average day in a normal, nonaddicted brain, the dopamine number hangs around 100. With a good meal, the dopamine level might rise to 150. With sex or morphine, it might rise to 200; with cigarettes, 225; with cocaine, 350; and with methamphetamines, 1,000. Wow! As you can see, drugs of abuse often produce dopamine surges that are many times higher than the surges produced by such natural rewards as food and sex, which is why drugs are so much more powerful and so much more destructive. Addiction starts as a problem of dopamine numbers in the reward circuitry of our limbic brain.

However, beyond making us feel good, dopamine is involved in a special type of learning known as conditioning or reward-driven learning. Because of dopamine, the context of the drug-use experience — the good times — adds value and strength to the drug memory. This added strength is what we call "salience." This "value-added" salient memory now has more power, holds a higher priority, and commands in us a stronger desire to seek the experience again, so we are driven to act in anticipation of the reward. In this way, the brain becomes addicted from a combination of repeated drug exposure and repeated reward-driven learning, both of which depend on the action of dopamine.

How does this relate to our three brains? Drugs activate and strengthen the "pleasure" response in the limbic brain, while weakening the fear response to potential harm in the reptilian brain and also reducing the inhibition exerted by the cortical brain — or the cortex, which governs decision making and executive functioning. The reduced cortical inhibition makes risky behaviors seem more rewarding and the harmful consequences less relevant, so that using drugs and its consequences become increasingly normal.

This becomes a negative spiral. Desire for the drug experience increases as it is repeated, and eventually this drives the reward circuitry completely out of control so that it takes over the entire brain system. In other words, our reward circuitry runs amok and cuts itself off, disconnecting itself from the control of the rational cortical brain and perhaps also the self-protective reptilian brain. That, in a nutshell, is how the brain acquires the disease of addiction. An addicted person might continue to function in society, to varying degrees of success, but their mind becomes obsessed with thinking about drugs, dreaming of drugs, remembering drug experiences, and using drugs. Once someone is addicted, this takeover of the mind continues despite the increasingly serious consequences of drug use.

Once the cortical brain is overridden, a person loses their inhibitory control. Thus, addiction is like losing the brakes in your car. Normally, your little sedan has pretty good brakes, but under the influence of drugs, your brake pedal will fail just as you pick up speed going down a very steep slope. An old Japanese proverb puts it this way:

First the man takes a drink,
Then the drink takes a drink,
Then the drink takes the man.

This process is the same no matter which drug leads to addiction. Underlying all addictions is the same brain

mechanism, which results in very similar behavioral manifestations and often common destructive consequences.
That said, different drugs are obviously experienced differently. In general, drugs affect the brain in one of four ways.
Stimulants like tobacco and cocaine enhance brain activity
by "kicking it up a notch," whereas depressants such as sed-
atives, benzodiazepines, and alcohol suppress brain activity. Psychedelics and hallucinogens completely muddle the
brain's working processes. Finally, opioids have a unique
way of affecting the brain. They are primarily prescribed to
kill pain, but it is more correct to say they reduce suffering.
Opioids don't actually eliminate pain, but the person feels
like nothing much matters. This is why the ancient Greeks
called opioids the "medicine of the gods": The gods on
Mount Olympus were far removed from and did not much
care about mortal troubles.

Of course, people become addicted to things besides
drugs. They can become addicted to food, sex, porn, gam-
bling, video games, the internet, and so on. Whatever the
cause, the core feature is the extreme takeover of all life
activities by the addictive behavior. The
addictive experience becomes the pre-
dominant driving force in the person's daily life — everything is
wrapped up in it, and everything is
ruined by it. Addiction is a disease
of extremes, and anything done to
extreme takes over everything else
and becomes a dominating fact of life.

> *Addiction is a
> disease of extremes, and
> anything done to extreme
> takes over everything else
> and becomes a dominating
> fact of life.*

Why Do People Take Drugs?

We have discussed how the brain works, how drugs affect the brain, how the brain becomes addicted, and how it stays addicted — as it learns and incorporates drug experiences into memory and as its reward circuitry overwhelms rational inhibitions. Now let's ask perhaps the most important question of all: Why do people take drugs in the first place?

Alan Leshner, former director of the National Institute on Drug Abuse, puts it simply: "People take drugs to feel good or to feel better." In other words, people take drugs because they like how the drugs make them feel. Since we all want to feel good, and we all want to feel better when we do not feel good, what's wrong with that?

Nothing, really. There's nothing wrong with wanting to feel good and be happy. After all, America's founding fathers put the pursuit of happiness, along with life and liberty, into the Declaration of Independence as one of our inalienable rights. What's the big fuss if people take drugs in pursuit of happiness?

Well, a few things. One is that the "good time" from drugs can become addicting, and being addicted is not a happy place. An addict doesn't do drugs to "pursue happiness," but out of compulsion. Further, and more importantly, the "happiness" people feel on drugs isn't the "happiness" that the founding fathers were talking about. The "happiness" referred to in the Declaration of Independence is related to "virtue." It's the kind of happiness you experience by becoming the person you want to be and by engaging in meaningful, productive activities that help others. In other words, the founding fathers meant the satisfaction of a successful life, feeling good from having done good, not pursuing personal pleasure for its own sake.

These two types of happiness are entirely different. They have different names, involve different brain mechanisms, and have very different effects on our health. Pleasure for its own sake — "having a good time" without any other meaning or purpose and benefiting only oneself — is called "hedonia." This type of happiness creates a physiological response that is similar to when the body is under stress: Excitement is accompanied by increases in blood pressure and respiration, by increases in blood sugar and stress hormones, and by a decrease in immune responses. Which is to say, as with stress, too much of this kind of happiness can make you sick — which is the price you pay for the good time.

The other kind of happiness — feeling good from personal satisfaction and from helping others and one's community through meaningful actions — is called "eudemonia." The physiological responses that accompany this feeling are the opposite of hedonia's: Blood pressure, respiration, blood sugar, and stress hormones all decrease, and immune-response hormones increase — in other words, you get healthier.

You may not be surprised to learn that these two types of happiness involve different parts of our brain. Hedonia, or personal pleasure, is antithetical to reflection; as we've discussed, the limbic brain's reward centers overwhelm the rational cortical brain — the part of our brain that makes us uniquely human. On the other hand, eudemonia emerges from self-reflection and self-awareness, and it requires the highest level of cortical brain function. In a way, with eudemonia we feel good about precisely what makes us uniquely human — like being a good worker, a good friend, or a good parent. That is what feeling good about yourself is all about.

PAUSE

Think back on specific times when you have felt happy. When have you felt hedonia, or personal pleasure, and when have you felt eudemonia, or happiness because of who you are? It's been said that eudemonia is the kind of happiness you want to tell your grandchildren about. What moments of happiness in your life would you want to share with your grandchildren?

Why do people do drugs? They seek hedonia, to feel good, and if they become addicted, they get stuck seeking hedonia and pay dearly for it, for addiction undermines feelings of eudemonia, or feeling good about the person you are.

Why Don't, or Can't, People Stop Taking Drugs?

This discussion of happiness begs the question: If someone isn't happy taking drugs, then why don't they just stop? Indeed, if someone can voluntarily stop taking drugs whenever they want and for however long they want, and they don't suffer mentally or physically after stopping, then almost by definition they are not addicted. But that is not what happens with addiction. The correct and more accurate question is why *can't* people just stop taking drugs when they want to? Many addicts do in fact want to stop taking drugs, but they can't. Addicted persons cannot simply stop taking drugs, because their addicted brain compels them to act like addicts. Their brain chemistry has changed, and the addict is literally not the same person they were before. For them, starting and stopping taking drugs is not like opening and closing a window. It's more like they have opened a bottle of soda; what's inside has become different, and they can't just put the cap back on and expect what's inside to return to the way it was before.

Further, becoming addicted is not the same as staying addicted. When a person first chooses to do drugs, the drug's effects and reward-driven learning reinforce the desire to repeat the drug experience. Early on, people often give in to their desire to do drugs again by telling themselves they can stop whenever they want. But in fact, continuing to do drugs steadily changes their brain so that it's harder to say no. Being unable to stop — such as relapsing even after going through detox — has more to do with how repetition has reinforced drug memories (which is discussed in chapter 2). To put it another way, someone becomes addicted because of the drug effects, but the person stays addicted because they remember those effects with a changed brain.

Likewise, getting off drugs is not the same as staying

off drugs. Getting off drugs — detoxification — focuses on ridding the body of drug effects. Staying off drugs — relapse prevention — means replacing drug memories with nondrug memories. This only happens by doing nondrug things over and over and over to build up a bank of nondrug memories. Over time, the brain develops a foundation of nondrug experiences, beliefs, and values that help the person make nonaddictive choices.

Overcoming addiction is mostly about staying off drugs — or relapse prevention. This is where we must direct every effort, and it's what the bulk of this book is about. In the end, we can sum up overcoming addiction in one sentence: It replaces the search for hedonic happiness with the effort to attain eudemonic happiness.

We can sum up overcoming addiction in one sentence: It replaces the search for hedonic happiness with the effort to attain eudemonic happiness.

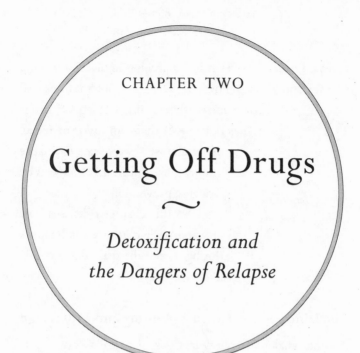

CHAPTER TWO

Getting Off Drugs

~

*Detoxification and
the Dangers of Relapse*

Getting off drugs — detoxification, or detox for short — is the first step in overcoming addiction. It is often said to be the first step in the journey of a thousand miles — the long journey of recovery, or living a sane and meaningful life without drugs. Detox is where everyone who tries to overcome addiction begins, and it is the most common addiction "treatment" offered in this country.

The sad truth is that detoxification is also where most people who try to overcome addiction stop. They fail to follow detox with relapse prevention, the necessary next step. Yes, detox is the first step in a journey of a thousand miles, but it is only one step. Alone, detox is not enough to overcome the dangers of relapse. Meanwhile, detoxification repeated over and over is like marching in place; it is not a journey and gets you nowhere. Detoxification may be good for a lot of things, but staying off drugs is not one of them. In my experience, detox almost always ends in relapse to drug use unless it is followed by relapse prevention.

Detoxification may be good for a lot of things, but staying off drugs is not one of them.

So this chapter discusses how to approach detox, what happens during it, and the main dangers that lead to relapse.

The Difference between a Wedding and a Marriage

Another analogy for how to think of detox — crude perhaps, but not necessarily bad — is to consider the difference between a wedding and a marriage.

Deciding to enter a detox program is the equivalent to becoming engaged — in a real way, the person commits to giving up the life of being single. The wedding ceremony is the detox program itself. Though it's no party, detox is also one of the biggest events of a person's life, and this commitment is not made in private. To some extent, it is a public pledge to change forever, one that is typically overseen by professionals and witnessed by the person's closest friends and family members.

Then what? Well, if you're getting married, after the wedding remains the rest of your life, and the ceremony doesn't have much to do with creating a successful marriage.

It doesn't matter whether the wedding is simple or lavish, indoors or out, formal or informal. It doesn't matter how much money you spend. Your wedding planner, and all the people you hire to get you through the ceremony, will move on to the next wedding, and after a brief honeymoon, you and your new spouse will be left to figure out how to be happy together and remain faithful. In other words, a successful married life depends on everything you do *after* the wedding. It depends entirely on the work you put in every day to create a satisfying life together. It depends on caring, loving, honest communication, through thick and thin, for better and for worse. The wedding is the promise of a lifelong commitment, but it's not the commitment itself.

It is the same with detox. During this ceremony, you get off drugs. But that is no guarantee you will stay off. How many people eventually divorce and become single again? Clearly, they were not ready to be married, or marriage was harder than they thought, or they chose the wrong person. To avoid relapse, you have to approach detox with the right attitude, and you've got to adopt this attitude before you get yourself to the church on time. Some people think they can have one last fix just before they give it all up and go into detox. That's like having one last fling before the wedding, and it doesn't bode well for what's to follow.

Detox is the first step toward changing your brain and changing your life. But it will take much more than detox to stay off drugs and build a new drug-free life.

PAUSE

The central ceremony of a wedding is the exchange of vows. What are your vows for recovery? Whether or not you've already been through detox, take a few moments and consider what you have pledged to yourself. If you wish, write this down and keep it as a reminder.

Detox Treatment and Medications

Detoxification, with or without medications, is the most common treatment for addiction offered and received in the United States. People can undergo detox almost anywhere: in an inpatient facility or outpatient clinic, an upscale residence or their own apartment. Whatever the context, the goal is the same: to remove the person from the constant bombardment of drug exposure, to give them some symptomatic relief from the physical and psychological discomfort of not having drugs anymore, and most importantly to give the brain time to recover from the effects of repeated drug exposure.

Detox is physically and mentally painful. It involves suffering, but it's a finite amount of suffering. It doesn't go on and on and on indefinitely; eventually it ends, usually lasting a matter of days to maybe a week or two. However, for this reason, it's almost never accomplished alone. The person going through detox needs physical and emotional support so as not to feel abandoned or have to face the ordeal alone. Misery loves company.

The use of medications in this setting is typically short term and only for relief of temporary symptoms, like physical aches and pains, anxiety, and sleep disturbances. An example of some typical medications are acetaminophen and ibuprofen for aches and pains. These medications are not meant to help you stay off drugs, though doctors might prescribe other medications for relapse prevention, which are continued after detox. See chapter 3 for more on the use of medications to prevent relapse.

Ultimately, however it's handled, the goal of detox is to bring the person back to "square one," where they can begin again.

What Happens during Detox

Detoxification sounds like ridding the body of some serious toxic stuff, but in reality it simply means letting the effects of the drugs wear off. Repeated exposure to drugs puts the body — especially the brain — under stress, and the body has to adjust to the effects of these drugs to keep going. Eventually, the body gets used to the drug effects by resetting itself, so that the effects of the drugs are the "new normal" — business as usual, if you will. In detox, the drugs are taken away, and the brain and body have to readjust again. This is stress on stress. That's why detox is tough, and why many people quit before they finish. Just remember, detox involves a finite amount of discomfort. The suffering will end.

At first, as the brain gets used to not dealing with the drug's effects, the person feels the opposite way they felt when they were stoned on drugs. The person doesn't feel "normal," the way they used to feel before becoming addicted. Withdrawal creates an opposite reaction. For instance, someone who used stimulants like methamphetamine or cocaine — which kick the brain up a notch — will now feel draggy and have no energy. Everything will be blah. Instead of feeling on top of the world, they will be down in the pits. If someone is addicted to alcohol or other depressants, then withdrawal will make them feel jittery and restless. They won't be able to calm down enough to figure out whether that noise is rain on the roof or the phone ringing. They won't be able to sleep and may wish someone would glue their eyelids together.

Opioids have a unique effect on the brain. They affect us powerfully, both physically and emotionally, but when we use them, we mostly feel the emotional effects: the feeling that nothing bothers us or even matters. However, in detox the physical effects become dominant. Withdrawal from opioids causes aches and pains, nausea and vomiting, cramps, diarrhea, chills, and goose bumps — which is why we call it going "cold turkey." The legs jerk as we kick the habit.

The good news is that all these symptoms pass eventually. A person may feel like they are dying, but withdrawal won't actually kill them — unless the person does something really stupid and dangerous while out of their head.

This is why most treatment facilities provide some medications during detox, to ease the symptoms of withdrawal.

Thus, in the early days of detox, the addict will actually become sicker, not healthier, as the drug effects wear off. This isn't that surprising given what we know about addiction. Remember, getting high with drugs puts the brain under stress: A person's heart rate and blood pressure go up, blood sugar spikes, cortisol and other stress hormones go up, and immune responses go down. You become sick; it's the price you pay for getting high. The brain eventually adjusts to accommodate these changes and keep things in balance. During detox, the brain has to do the reverse. With no drugs to compensate for, the brain readjusts to the neurophysiological changes, and that puts more stress on a brain system that is already run-down.

This is what makes the first days of treatment such a critical and difficult period in recovery, and this is why people undergoing detoxification have such a tough time participating meaningfully in recovery. Patients and families must not become discouraged by this seeming lack of progress, and doctors and other caregivers must not regard this reaction as a patient's lack of motivation. Patience is key all around. Detox is just a tough time for everyone to get through. It may sound strange, but there is wisdom in the old clinical folklore: "Drug them, don't bug them." Meaning, let medications ease symptoms, and give the person time.

While specific withdrawal symptoms vary with different drugs, the mechanism of stress is the same. All drug exposures place similar demands on the brain to adapt. The extent of drug exposure and the severity of addiction are what determine the magnitude of the brain changes and the severity of withdrawal symptoms.

Neurochemically speaking, this phase of detoxification is defined by chronically elevated stress hormones — adrenaline and noradrenaline, cortisol, and amygdala CRF (corticotrophin releasing factor) — which are expressed clinically as anxiety, depression, irritability, loss of energy and interest, and general lassitude. Drugs, cues, and everyday stress trigger intense craving and drug memories. Sleep is fitful and everything has a negative overtone to it. All this happens on top of a neural circuitry that is already "stressed-out," oversensitive to further stress, and sluggish to cortical control. No wonder the user often wishes to return to drug-induced oblivion, and not surprisingly, relapse is common.

Meanwhile, the period immediately following acute withdrawal is most characterized by anhedonia — a sense of purposelessness and the inability to experience pleasure. The brain is "burned-out" and needs to recharge. This is what we mean when we say the addicted brain needs to heal. Medications can help relieve certain symptoms, such as anxiety, depression, and sleep disturbance, and they can help cope with stress, but what the exhausted brain needs most is time to heal in a healthy environment. Healthy body, healthy brain, so to speak. Hopefully, understanding these neurobiological underpinnings will help the user persevere through the difficult days of detox and move forward to the next phase, the core in overcoming addiction: relapse prevention.

However, there is a final danger once detox is over and the person is enjoying the afterglow of relief. Things will feel so different and so much better that the person may fall into the trap of thinking that things will remain better from now on. They may fool themselves into believing the hard work is over when it has really only just begun. These good feelings are only a temporary honeymoon phase. In order to stay off drugs, the person must focus on building a new life immediately. The two are so intensely intertwined that one cannot succeed without the other. You can't stay off drugs for long if you don't build a sane and meaningful other-centered life, one that is based on consideration of people besides yourself; and you cannot build a sane and meaningful life if you don't stay off drugs.

The rest of this chapter discusses the most common reasons people relapse after detox.

You can't stay off drugs for long if you don't build a sane and meaningful other-centered life, one that is based on consideration of people besides yourself; and you cannot build a sane and meaningful life if you don't stay off drugs.

What Is Relapse?

As I've said, there is a huge difference between becoming addicted and being addicted. Once someone is addicted, the repeated drug use creates lasting changes in the brain

— from repeated reward-driven learning and memory, or conditioning — that leads to a compulsion to use drugs. The addicted person cannot "not use" when drugs are available. Even when someone succeeds in getting off drugs, or completes detox, their addiction remains and will undermine efforts to stay off drugs. This is why the most common outcome of detoxification — by whatever means, whether from hospitalization or incarceration — is relapse.

Relapse is not the same as becoming addicted for the first time. It may look the same on the surface — a person who is not using drugs starts taking them — but what happens in the brain with relapse is entirely different, and it does not feel the same to the addict, either.

The first time someone takes a drug, their brain is essentially normal. It has not yet been repeatedly exposed to the drug, and it has not yet learned to associate how the drug makes them feel with the context of the drug experiences and to encode those into drug-use memories. However, someone with an addiction can't feel normal without the drug, and they relapse not so much to "feel good" but to "feel normal." In other words, their brain has become diseased from repeated drug exposure and drug experiences, and these changes are permanently stored as memories in the brain. These memories and associations must be dealt with, difficult though that may be, if relapse is to be prevented and addiction is to be overcome.

After detox, the real challenge to staying off drugs is that these memories are continually renewed and reinforced by reminders, or triggers, that are everywhere. Staying off drugs is hard in the same way that forgetting a lost love, or any strong memory, is hard. Eubie Blake's song "Memories of You" captures this well:

> Waking skies at sunrise, every sunset too,
> Seems to be bringing me memories of you.
> Here and there, everywhere, scenes that we once knew,
> And they all just recall memories of you.
> How I wish I could forget those happy yesteryears
> That have left a rosary of tears.
> Your face beams in my dreams, 'spite of all I do!
> Everything seems to bring memories of you.

Dealing with a brain disease is a real challenge. It takes hard work, which is why most of this book focuses on relapse prevention. First, let us explore the events that lead to a relapse.

The Three Ingredients of a Relapse

There are three ingredients of a relapse: drug memories, triggers (which include drugs, cues, and stress), and emotional buildup. These three elements work together like a stage play. Drug memories are the story line — the familiar scenes. The triggers are the players, and the emotional buildup is the dialogue. Ultimately, the only way to change this drama is to rewrite the script, which is the focus of chapters 3 through 8.

Memories

Drug memories drive relapses. Another analogy is that drug memories are like seeds buried in the soil ready to sprout when the rain comes. While avoiding triggers and emotional buildup is important, those two elements wouldn't be an issue without drug memories. They would be like players with no lines to say.

Because of conditioning, or reward-driven learning, old drug experiences become heightened memories with added power and higher priority. They arouse a sense of longing and an irresistible desire or craving to relive the drug experience. Rationally, a recovering addict knows that doing drugs will be harmful, but that doesn't stop the craving. As in the Eubie Blake song, it's like remembering the spark of an old romance, which ignites an irresistible urge to see that person again, even though the romance ended painfully.

The sudden reappearance of drugs, seeing things connected to doing drugs, and even everyday stress can bring back old drug memories. Once the memories are recalled, the person wishes for the comfort of the "good old days," even though those "good old days" ruined their life. We call this process regression, and it might be compared to a longing to return to the comfort of the womb. It's the desire to feel safe and protected from suffering at all costs.

Triggers

Triggers are what recall the drug memories, those ruinous "good old days." Anything can summon a drug memory, but the most common triggers are drugs and paraphernalia, cues, and stress. We call them triggers because they initiate a chain of events that can lead the recovering addict to relapse.

Once triggered, drug memories are rehearsed and reenacted in the emotional brain, so that the memories become present, as if they are being relived. It is a bit like what happens when you hear an old, familiar tune. You can hear just three notes, and for the rest of the evening, the tune repeats over and over in your head. If you have strong emotions associated with the tune, this can put you under the spell of that mood. Just a glimpse of a Marlboro Man cigarette ad will make someone crave to smoke. If you have an allergy, something can trigger a sneezing fit and be gone in a minute, but your nose will still run for hours afterward. Triggers are like that. Once you start recalling drug memories, it's hard to stop.

Drugs and Paraphernalia

Drugs and paraphernalia are the most obvious triggers. It is important to get rid of them early in recovery. Don't say to yourself, "I can put them away, and they won't bother me when I get stronger." This is self-deception.

One common misunderstanding is the belief that craving occurs because the addict cannot get drugs. Actually, the opposite is true — addicts crave drugs when they know they *can* get them. In fact, craving subsides when the addict knows for certain that drugs are not available.

For example, I knew a heroin addict who went through

detox in a secure facility where drugs were unavailable. He soon stopped craving heroin and stopped having signs and symptoms of withdrawal for months. Eventually, he felt normal and looked just like anyone else. Later, he was released from the facility because he seemed to have gotten over his drug habit. After being released, he took a bus back into town. As soon as the bus got to his old neighborhood, his nose started running, his eyes began tearing, and he started to crave heroin. This happened not because he lacked drugs but because for the first time since he'd quit he knew he could get them again. His old dealer lived just around the corner. The potential ability to get drugs triggered his drug memories, and as he relived them, the craving returned.

> One common misunderstanding is the belief that craving occurs because the addict cannot get drugs. Actually, the opposite is true — addicts crave drugs when they know they *can* get them.

This is why it is so important for addicts in recovery to avoid known triggers. Get rid of your stash, your paraphernalia, and your drug-using friends, and replace those things with new activities and new friends. As the following chapters discuss, this is how you replace the old drug memories with non-drug-using memories.

Cues

Cues are a major concern for relapse prevention because they are everywhere. While there are plenty of external cues — sights, sounds, smells, tastes, people, places, music, movies, food, drinks, friends, bars, and more — there are many internal cues as well, especially feelings of depression, anger, and anxiety. These feelings are so common that we are probably experiencing one of them most of the time. We often feel sad, mad, or afraid about something, so it is virtually impossible to prevent these internal cues, no matter how hard we try. It makes good common sense to avoid external cues as much as possible, but more important is learning how to handle all cues, internal and external, whenever they arise, which later chapters address.

Stress
"Everything is a hassle!"

Every day we feel stress, but learning to deal with stress requires a better understanding of what it really means. Stress arises from not knowing what to do or from feeling helpless, but knowing what to do depends on what we have, and have not, learned. For addicts, stress arises from the things they did while doing drugs, and it arises from things they didn't do but should have done during that same time. Initiation to drug use most often happens in adolescence, and in those cases addicts not only learn a lot of bad habits while using, but they also miss opportunities to mature and grow into adulthood. Both of these cause stress.

Addicts are frequently admonished to "get a life!" The problem is that they got an addict's life. To learn to live a nonaddicted life, they must unlearn their old habits while acquiring new, healthy habits. This in itself is very stressful. Developing habits requires learning, memory, and practice.

To "get a new life" requires learning and practicing new ways of being to build new memories to replace the old, ingrained ones. This is hard work, and hard work leads to stress. As with cues, the goal isn't so much to avoid stress as to learn how to deal with it when it arises.

PAUSE

Think about your current habits. Which would you say are good habits, which neutral, and which bad? Identify a few habits you know you need to change, and keep them in mind as you read. How long do you think it takes to change or create a habit? Find the answer in this book.

Emotional Buildup

Memories and triggers set the stage for relapse. They represent the story line and the players. The emotional buildup is what I consider the play itself. It represents the internal dialogue of the addict — or the conversation between the players, if you will — that moves someone from "readiness" to an actual return to drug use. Emotional buildup is the final step in relapse.

These internal conversations have one goal: to make returning to drug use seem acceptable, natural, and even justifiable. It may seem counterintuitive that someone who has gone through detox would talk themselves back into using, but this is made possible by the addiction itself. The addict has become accustomed, consciously and unconsciously, to all the behaviors that maintaining an addiction requires. For example, addicts are used to lying, cheating, stealing, failing to keep appointments and promises, neglecting personal responsibilities (such as maintaining health and self-care), and failing to take a responsible role in the community. In one way or another, these behaviors and bad habits may continue into the present, and they make relapse seem natural.

In other words, the emotional buildup involves all the rationalizations a person uses to convince themselves to return to drug use. Here are some common ones that may sound familiar.

Nobody cares anyway. I might as well use.

I was cleaning my house and found some heroin I had forgotten about.

I was at a party, and someone offered me drugs. What could I do?

I lost my job, so why not use?

I need to use so that I can feel more comfortable around people.

I can't enjoy sex without drugs.

I can't relax after a stressful day without heroin.

The only time I don't feel depressed is when I use.

The rationalizations above reflect reactions to negative emotions and unexpected events, but early in recovery, someone may also become overconfident. They may feel they've mastered their addiction, or they want to test themselves and prove they are stronger than drugs. They may convince themselves that they can use again just once or just a little. This is wrong. It is very easy to forget that the key to preventing relapse is to create a new, drug-free life, not becoming "stronger" than addiction. Here are some rationalizations that arise from overconfidence:

> I haven't used in a long time. I'm sure I can stop this time.
>
> I'm strong enough to be around it now. I want to see if I can say "no" to using.
>
> Now I'm in control, and I can stop when I want to.
>
> I will use only small amounts and only once in a while.
>
> This drug was not my problem, but another one; I can use this one and not relapse.
>
> I'm really feeling good. One time won't hurt.
>
> Things are going great. I owe myself a reward.
>
> This is such a special event, and there is only one way to celebrate.

PAUSE

Consider what drug memories, triggers, cues, and stressful situations might lead to emotional buildup for you. What triggers are easy to avoid, and which will be hard or impossible to avoid? What strategies could you use to remind yourself when rationalizations crop up? Keep these ideas in mind as you read.

If you find that you have used some of these rationalizations in the past, don't dwell on it. The past cannot be changed. The only way to temper these feelings is to have a set of nonaddictive behaviors to draw on, which is what the rest of this book helps you with. However, it is very important to learn to recognize triggers and emotional buildup as they occur and to nip them in the bud. A small urge can be stopped, but stopping becomes more difficult as the urge grows. Avoid known triggers as much as possible, and when a trigger is encountered, practice stopping negative thinking and self-talk the moment they begin.

A few techniques that may seem silly but can help stop triggers before they grow into something unmanageable include snapping your fingers, snapping a rubber band, and switching to a different channel of thought. Then, to counter emotional buildup and rationalizations, get up and do something: Call a friend or your counselor (if you have one), exercise, talk to someone in your family, or write in your diary.

Remember, avoiding triggers and learning to reduce stress are all part of the relapse prevention strategy.

You Can't Forget, So Stop Using and Start Living

If addicts could get rid of their drug memories, they would not relapse. For instance, longtime cigarette smokers have been known to simply stop smoking after suffering an accident that destroyed the memory centers in their brain. They couldn't remember what it was like to smoke, so they didn't smoke. Scientists are researching how to wipe out certain memories, or modify them, without destroying important parts of the brain, and findings from this work have been useful in treating patients with brain conditions such as post-traumatic stress disorder. Still, we are a long way from having a simple treatment that would eliminate drug-use memories. So, for now, we have to deal with relapse prevention the old-fashioned way: by creating a nondrug life and accumulating nondrug memories.

As this chapter explains, triggers cause the recovering addict to replay drug memories, and reliving these drug memories can lead to cravings and urges to use drugs, which build up until the addict rationalizes using drugs again as "acceptable," expected, and natural. The stepwise development of this process is important, but equally important is understanding that the longer the process goes on, the greater the chance that it will lead to an undesirable conclusion — in other words, to relapse.

The primary ways to overcome the urge to relapse include recognizing and combating drug cues and triggers, avoiding drugs and resisting drug offers, dealing with craving, and stopping addictive thoughts and emotional buildup. Obviously, that's easier said than done. In fact, accomplishing this may seem overwhelming. You might think that it is asking a lot, and you are right. To stay off drugs, you have to rebuild your life. Successfully getting off drugs, or completing detoxification, is a great accomplishment. You should take pride in it and feel really good about yourself. By getting off drugs, you wipe the slate clean and bring yourself back to square one. But life doesn't hold still. You have to move forward. Where and how you move forward from square one determine whether you will successfully walk a different path of life without drugs.

CHAPTER THREE

Getting to Sanamluang, or Preparing for a New Life

Relapse Prevention

I grew up in Bangkok, Thailand, and next to the Royal Palace is a big oval playing field the locals call Sanamluang — "royal ground." When the country was an absolute monarchy, this was the exclusive playground for the royal family, and afterward it was opened to the public. Today it hosts a great open-air market on weekends that is a huge tourist attraction, and it has become a favorite gathering place for locals, especially schoolchildren and their parents. The huge greenspace is perfect for many recreational activities and sports, like soccer and kite flying and kite fighting. It is a place where you meet your best friends on Saturday mornings to plan how to spend the day having fun. Nothing really gets planned until you get to Sanamluang.

Over time, the term "getting to Sanamluang" has come to signify starting over. On the surface, it may seem a waste that you have to go somewhere just to start over, but the point of a "starting place" is that it gives you a chance to assess where you want to go and perhaps choose a different, better direction. In Bangkok, if you are having trouble with your girlfriend, for example, you have to "get to Sanamluang" to make up.

The Western version of "getting to Sanamluang" is "going back to square one." It's interesting how these sayings reflect different cultural attitudes to "starting over." To Thais, "getting to Sanamluang" means moving forward, getting somewhere, making progress. In the West, "square one" means going backward. No wonder we in the West become discouraged when we have to go back to square one. Really, we should rethink that. We shouldn't underestimate the power of square one. Starting points define our journey. In this place, we truly know where we stand, and from here we can plot our new direction and measure our progress. It is a place of renewed hope and new action, where old ruinous memories can be left behind and new constructive ones created.

We shouldn't underestimate the power of square one. Starting points define our journey.

The Power of Square One

Remember, the whole purpose of detoxification is to provide you with the opportunity and freedom to pursue a new, sane, meaningful life without drugs. Detoxification gets you to Sanamluang. The power of square one is that, from here, you get to decide what your new life will look like. So, what do you want it to be?

Ultimately, building a drug-free life and relapse prevention are two sides of the same coin. They are so intimately linked that one doesn't exist without the other. Succeed at one, and you automatically succeed at both.

To begin, consider the two types of happiness I describe in chapter 1: hedonia, or personal pleasure, and eudemonia, or being happy because of who you are. A sane and meaningful life flows from an other-centered worldview, in which true happiness comes not from having a good time, but from doing something good for others, which is what makes us feel good about ourselves. If we use the pursuit of eudemonia as our guide, then every time we feel it we will know we are closer to achieving our ultimate goal, a meaningful life. Focus on that every day, first by improving your personal life and then by helping others in their lives, and step-by-step you will reach your destination.

Or, to use different terms, to achieve a productive and meaningful life, you must replace the old drug-use memories with new nondrug memories by doing things differently, and these memories form the basis of new nondrug behaviors and self-sustaining habits. This takes energy and effort. Confucius once said that to rule the universe, you must first ready yourself, then put your house in order, then govern the country, and then conquer the world. Of course, our goal isn't world domination but ruling our personal universe. To do so, you must plan and prepare, then take personal responsibility for your actions, and then do what's necessary to live the life that you intend, ultimately in ways that contribute to your community.

Not long ago a group of addiction experts meeting at the Betty Ford Center concluded that recovery is a lifestyle characterized by abstinence, health, and citizenship — taking personal responsibility and becoming a responsible member of the community. The first step in recovery, once you get off drugs and are ready to start a new life, is to take better care of your health. This gives you the energy to do all the things you want and need to do. Equally important is having sound emotional health. As we will discuss, three common destructive emotions that sap energy and put someone in danger of relapse are anxiety, anger, and depression. Learning to handle these is vital. You also must live up to the obligations of everyday life — earning an income, paying bills — and build trust in your relationships: with family, friends, coworkers, and others. The basic bond of trust gives rise to hope, and hope is what a responsible person gives to others and to oneself. When people turn to you for help, they don't do so because you are a genius. Rather, they know you can be counted on to help in whatever way you can. They trust you!

Learning to take personal responsibility isn't always hard, but it can frequently be humbling. However, it's what growing up is about. The good news is that, wherever you are in your life, and no matter how much you feel you may have missed while you were addicted to drugs, you can still learn everything you need to. In fact, now that you're older, you will learn faster. Unlike a teenager, who has experienced very little of life, as an adult in recovery, you have experienced a lot. As you uncover the wisdom in your experience, you may have many "wow" or "eureka" moments, when you make connections that lead to sudden realizations. These flashes of insight — the word "eureka" means "I have found it," and it is attributed to the ancient Greek scholar Archimedes, who shouted it in his bathtub — may not happen every day, and they don't need to. Rather, if you keep yourself focused on what's most important, if you keep paying attention and cultivating eudemonia, you can learn quickly and steadily create the life you want.

PAUSE

Consider for a moment what starting over means to you. Do you feel it's a positive or negative place? Imagine you are standing at "square one." What new, different directions could you take in your life as you move forward?

Eight Steps to Building a Balanced and Meaningful Life

The term "relapse prevention" states what you don't want to do, that is, drugs. But building a meaningful life is defined by the opposite: It's the result of what you do, the positive actions you take. The rest of this book will focus on what you can do to proactively create a balanced and meaningful life. These are the activities that build a new memory bank to replace the old relapse-prone set of drug-related memories. This is what keeps you off drugs.

To help discuss this complex topic, I've broken relapse prevention into eight steps. However, in practice, these steps cannot be neatly pigeonholed. They overlap; each step supports and is related to the others. One step doesn't automatically lead to the next, nor do they need to be followed in any particular order. It can help to approach these topics one at a time, but the ultimate goal is to practice these steps together, all the time.

If this list sounds like a lot to expect, don't become discouraged. There are a lot of things to learn, but the more you practice, the easier it all becomes.

Step 1 (chapter 3). Plan ahead and be proactive: create a schedule, take medications as needed, seek support, and stay busy developing good habits.

Step 2 (chapter 4). Ready yourself physically: develop healthy routines of nutrition, hygiene, exercise, rest, meditation, and sleep.

Step 3 (chapter 5). Ready yourself mentally: develop mindfulness; practice overcoming anger, loneliness, guilt, and shame; distinguish being smart from being strong.

Step 4 (chapter 6). **Take care of business:** get a job, return to school, develop a career.

Step 5 (chapter 6). **Act responsibly:** stay out of jail, stay on the job, pay your bills.

Step 6 (chapter 7). **Live harmoniously with family and friends:** repair damaged relationships, build trust, make new friends.

Step 7 (chapter 8). **Be a good member of the community:** be a friend, help others, give back.

Step 8 (chapter 9). **Maintain a balanced and meaningful life:** seek meaning and spirituality.

The number 8 in Chinese means "blessing" and is a highly regarded number. It is a symbol of "perfection." For instance, the number 8 is perfectly balanced whether you divide it vertically or horizontally. Even if you are not into Chinese culture, you might still consider these eight steps as containing the blessing of a meaningful life. See the specific chapters noted above for fuller explanations of each step and how to achieve it.

From Chaos to Order: Planning a New Life

What characterizes the life of an addict is chaos. As a prerequisite to building a new life from scratch, you have to bring order to this chaos. It is like the first thing that must happen after demolition — in this case, wiping the slate clean by getting off drugs through detox. A new drug-free life won't just happen; addicts do not stay off drugs just because they want to. Something needs to fill the empty lot where drug addiction used to be, but before you start building, you need architectural drawings that show contractors what to build. In other words, you need a plan.

As you read the rest of this book, consider all the positive things that you want and need to do to create a meaningful life. How will you fill the time that was once devoted to addiction? You don't need to think of everything right away, but you need to start somewhere. Focus first on personal actions closest to home: eating a balanced diet, practicing good hygiene, getting regular exercise, getting enough sleep, and so on. Consider joining support groups, repairing relationships, making new friendships, and taking care of business: your income, your job, your home.

Initially, also focus on removing from your life anything having to do with your previous addictive lifestyle: Get rid of drug paraphernalia, avoid drug dealers and drug-using friends, and avoid risky drug-related behavior. Learn and practice drug-refusing techniques, and cultivate an attitude and lifestyle of abstinence from all drugs of abuse, legal or not.

As you list all the things you need to accomplish, pull out a calendar and schedule each one by the day and the hour. When are you going to shop, work, make that phone call, see that friend, attend meetings? Ultimately, the goal of planning is to schedule nondrug activities for every waking hour of every day. Do this, and there will be no time or opportunity to relapse.

Scheduling may seem simple or even silly, but it gives your new life structure. A schedule is your architectural plan. Of course, it will change over time, and you will often need to be flexible. But don't be lax about planning. Be proactive. Every Sunday, plan each week; every morning, plan each day. Regard a blank square on the calendar as a problem to solve.

Why? Because relapse often begins when someone has nothing to do and nowhere to go. Being sober can start to feel boring, which is a frequent complaint among people who first stop using drugs. But the mind can't really be idle and focus on nothing for very long. If we're bored, our mind wanders until it attaches itself to something more interesting. If an addict's mind wanders to using, then these memories can start the craving process, and once an addict starts craving, this feeling can build till it leads to relapse. This is why we say that an idle mind is the devil's workshop, and "Bargains and compromises now; hell to pay later." Make sure you are too busy pursuing a meaningful life to be bored.

Also keep this in mind: If you fill up all your waking hours with things to do that do not include using drugs, when the day is over, you will have one whole day without using. That is one day of being drug-free. Repeat this enough times, and it becomes a habit. Repeat this habit, and it becomes your lifestyle. Do that, and you have overcome addiction.

PAUSE

How often do you feel bored? What do you do about it? Did you ever once do drugs simply out of boredom? Here's a plan for the next time you find yourself bored: Pledge to do the most difficult task on your to-do list. If you do, I guarantee life will suddenly be less boring.

Medications for Relapse Prevention

In chapter 2, I talked briefly about the role medications can play during detoxification. Similarly, medications can play a role in relapse prevention, or helping you stay off drugs of addiction. Several have been approved by the US Food and Drug Administration (FDA) for alcohol and for opioids. While it's beyond the scope of this book to discuss these medications in detail — plus, new medications are constantly being developed — the important thing to know is that effective medications are available, and you should talk to your doctor about whether they would help in your case.

Some recovering addicts refuse to take drugs of any kind; they regard all drugs, even helpful medications, as bad. However, I suggest keeping an open mind and avoiding any extreme views. Remember, the brain is, to a large extent, a chemical machine, and all medications work to change brain chemistry. While addiction is brain chemistry gone wrong, some medications can change brain chemistry for the better.

It's important not to reject medications out of hand, just as it's important to evaluate all medications carefully and to distinguish misinformation from real information. Don't be afraid to ask questions, and be cautious of anyone who is too certain about what they tell you.

Here are a few things to keep in mind.

1. Some medications are approved by the FDA for certain specific indications, which means they have been shown to be safe and effective for that purpose. At the moment, such medications exist for alcohol and for opioids, but none exist for cocaine or methamphetamine.

2. Physicians can use an FDA-approved medication for something not specifically indicated if there is enough support from the literature and experience that such use is effective and safe. These are known as "off-label" uses.

3. Be suspicious of any use of unapproved medications; always ask questions.

4. Remember there are no right or wrong medications; only the right or wrong ways to use a medication, any medication.

5. Taking a medication is not like taking a drug of abuse. Remember that addiction is not taking drugs; addiction is taking drugs and acting like an addict. If taking a medication doesn't make someone act like an addict, then it is not the same thing.

People often ask how long they have to keep taking these medications to prevent relapse. This is a legitimate concern, and the usual answer is, it depends. These medications are meant to help prevent relapse, and if you have been taking one of these medications and you have not used any street drugs, you have achieved half of the goal of building a sane, meaningful, nondrug life. People typically want to quit these medications as soon as possible, but the main risk is quitting too soon. The time to quit is only after you have archived a good measure of stable, meaningful drug-free experiences (as described in this book). When all is said and done, what relapse-prevention medications give you is freedom from a constant preoccupation with drugs so that you can devote your time to building a fulfilling life. Don't be too quick to give up your liberty.

What relapse-prevention medications give you is freedom from a constant preoccupation with drugs so you can devote your time to building a fulfilling life. Don't be too quick to give up your liberty.

Support Groups and Mentors

Unfortunately, in our current treatment system, recovering addicts are too often left to their own devices. However, no one can prevent relapse and build a meaningful life alone. You must seek and ask for support and help from others. In terms of relapse prevention, the most common strategy is to see a therapist or join a recovery group, such as Alcoholics

Anonymous and similar groups. There is nothing wrong with this and much to recommend it. It can be very helpful to talk with others who know firsthand what you are going through.

That said, groups and therapy are not for everyone. They require commitment and effort, just like anything, and not everyone is equally comfortable in them. Plus, each therapist and group is different. There is no one-size-fits-all in this. It may take several attempts before someone finds the right forum or the right people. The most important advice is to try a few sessions with a therapist or group and judge for yourself. If attending these sessions makes you feel like staying off drugs and doing something meaningful, keep going. If not, stop and try a different group or something else.

However, don't stop there. Consider people you know — either in your life or in history — whose actions and life inspire you and are worth emulating. We all learn from others, and they don't need to be formal teachers. Ideally, you can identify someone in your life who would be willing to be a mentor for you during recovery, someone you like and look up to and whom you can converse with easily. But we can also learn something from nearly everyone we come into contact with, as well as from historical figures and even fictional characters. Confucius said, "Whenever three people walk together, one of them is a teacher of mine." What he meant was that we can learn from just about everyone, whether we admire what they've done or not. It is all learning.

It doesn't even matter if the person you admire is alive or even real. When faced with uncertainty, you might reflect, "What would my hero do in this situation?" Asking questions like this can help you do the right thing and avoid lots of trouble. In the same vein, you might say to yourself, "I don't want to do anything that I wouldn't want my mother to find out about."

Others don't have to have shared our experience to help us. One mystery about learning is that we can apply knowledge in one area to many other, seemingly unrelated situations. This is called generalization, and it applies to our own knowledge. Faced with a unique situation, we do not have to learn everything from scratch. Everything in our brain is connected to everything else; our brains can connect what we already know to novel problems and figure out solutions. Telescopes can study both the constellations and the seas, the stars and the dolphins leaping out of the water.

In other words, never feel alone. Seek help, look to others for guidance, and trust that you can also be a good teacher to yourself.

PAUSE

Think about the people you admire, and name the qualities that you admire in them. Which of those qualities would help you most right now, and in what situations? Consider asking these people for support, even just in your mind, whenever you need it.

From Experience to Habit to Expertise:
Strength of Memory

As I say, relapse prevention depends on replacing old, drug-use memories with new, nondrug memories. What does that mean in practice?

What we do constitutes our life experience, which is what our memory is composed of. Doing things creates new brain connections, new protein syntheses, and new gene expressions that are stored as memories. Memory determines how we think and how we feel, and memories underlie our belief system. Our belief system determines how we act. How we act determines how things turn out in our lives.

That said, not all memories are equal. The strength of a memory increases as the experience that created the memory is repeated. At some point, a memory can grow so strong that it compels us to repeat the initial act effortlessly, as if it were automatic. It becomes a habit. When a habit forms, it indicates that the experience has been repeated a lot. When we call addictive behaviors "habits," we mean the addict is doing drugs and engaging in drug-related activities so much, often to the exclusion of virtually everything else, that they become automatic.

How much is "a lot"? How many repetitions do you need to make a habit? When people say "practice makes perfect," how much practice are they talking about?

Creating a habit takes somewhere from sixty to a few hundred repetitions, depending on the activity. At that point, the activity is done without thinking, and in some cases it becomes hard *not* to do the activity. Support groups are not kidding you when they tell you to go to ninety meetings in ninety days. Going to meetings once a week will not make this a habit.

If you think about it, addicts are experts at what they do. They spend thousands of hours practicing addictive behaviors — not just looking for drugs and using drugs but cheating, lying, stealing, and everything else that goes with life as an addict. So to overcome addiction, a person must seek to become a different kind of expert. They must pursue nonaddict activities just as relentlessly, repeating nonaddict life experiences over and over, day after day, until their memory grows strong enough for those actions to become automatic, matters of habit. Some have estimated that to become an expert, such as a good golfer or a good pianist, you must practice ten thousand hours and more. Bill Gates, the founder of Microsoft, practiced computer programming for well over ten thousand hours before he created his company. Success doesn't just happen.

To successfully overcome addiction, plan ahead, schedule your time, seek support, and then every hour of every day focus on the nondrug activities and nonaddictive behaviors described in the rest of this book, until pursuing a meaningful, nondrug life becomes not just your habit, but your area of expertise.

CHAPTER FOUR

Physical Health

~

We need sound physical health to successfully overcome addiction. For one thing, the life changes that overcoming addiction requires take great effort and energy, the foundation of which is physical health. Of course, mental health is important, too; as I have said, addiction is a brain disease. But a healthy brain needs a healthy body to support it. Consider that a full 20 percent of the body's blood is supplied to the brain, even though the brain represents only 2 percent of our body weight. Take those percentages to heart. You won't go wrong by emphasizing your physical health, since this directly supports your mental and emotional health.

There is another important reason to prioritize physical health. When addicts spend all their time getting drugs and getting high, they tend to neglect things like appearance, grooming, and personal hygiene. They don't make time for these things because their personal appearance often doesn't mean much. Indeed, addicts may not think very much of themselves at all, tending to have little self-esteem and self-respect. To start over and build a new, meaningful, nondrug life, the first thing to do is to rebuild one's self-worth. Being healthy and looking good are important signs that people like and respect themselves, and starting with these creates a virtuous circle: The more you care about and respect yourself, the more important your health becomes and, in turn, the more you will like and respect yourself.

Thus, physical health fosters eudemonia, or being happy about who you are, and as I've discussed, pursuing healthy habits and exercise creates just the sort of nondrug memories that support a nondrug life. Or, to put it another way, once you're at square one, the best guarantee to having your life turn out differently is to do things differently. If, while addicted, you neglected your physical health, then do the opposite now. Remember, activities become experiences, repeated experiences become habits, and habits become a lifestyle. Begin by taking care of yourself.

Scheduling a Healthy Lifestyle

In chapter 3, I discussed the importance of planning ahead, managing your time, and scheduling all your activities. Nowhere is this more important than for physical health, which requires daily maintenance. A healthy lifestyle is frequently a well-structured lifestyle. As this chapter makes clear, physical health depends on doing a lot of things, and you will need to plan ahead to take care of them all.

For instance, this chapter discusses abstinence from drugs, proper nutrition, adequate exercise, sufficient sleep, fatigue and illness management, and the importance of play and having fun. Good health means preventative care — getting regular medical and dental checkups — which means finding doctors and making appointments. Proper nutrition means shopping for food, cooking, and cleaning up. Looking good means getting a haircut and buying new clothes. A regular exercise program means, for example, finding a biking or jogging path, joining a gym or class, and at times coordinating with friends.

It may seem overwhelming to do all these things at once, so decide what is most important to you and begin there. Remember the aphorisms "one day at a time" and "every day, in every way, I am getting better and better" (attributed to the French psychologist Émile Coué).

That said, there is an important side benefit of working hard to maintain your physical health and appearance: It keeps you busy, and staying busy is a big part of relapse prevention. Busyness keeps you from becoming bored. In fact, one of the quickest and easiest ways to solve the problem of boredom is to take a walk. Every waking hour of the day, when you aren't doing something else, do something that improves your physical health. Sports and exercise are constructive, are often fun, and keep the mind in focus.

PAUSE

Research shows that people who feel good about them-selves are more attractive to others, since feeling good releases hormones that promote bonding. Since we all want to feel attractive, what are some things you can do to improve your self-esteem?

Total Abstinence Buys You Time

For your treatment to be truly effective, you must stop *all* drug and alcohol use, and I recommend that if you smoke cigarettes, you quit these as well. Total abstinence is the best approach to avoid relapse, since it buys you the time you need to develop nondrug memories and overcome addiction.

However, addicts often believe that having a problem with one drug does not mean they cannot continue to use other drugs in moderation, such as alcohol or marijuana. They may feel that their addiction is specific to a certain drug and that other drugs are not a problem. This is mostly untrue. Research clearly shows that continuing to use some drugs while learning to abstain from another drug creates roadblocks in the recovery process. Addicts in recovery who continue to use alcohol are also at a high risk for developing alcohol dependence. Furthermore, impaired judgment as a result of being intoxicated on alcohol can lead to relapse to other drug use.

Finally, research shows that a person's motivation or reasons for overcoming addiction have little bearing on whether they will be able to lead a drug-free lifestyle. You might think that someone who wants to stop using drugs for themselves would be more successful at maintaining abstinence than someone who was mandated to do so, but this has not proved to be the case. Instead, what is most important is the amount of time the recovering addict stays drug-free. Addicts must stay drug-free long enough to appreciate the benefits of a different lifestyle. After some period of abstinence, and after things have changed for the better — debts are no longer overwhelming, relationships have become more rewarding, work is going well, and health is good — a person is more likely to want to stay drug-free.

Nutrition: Eating Right and Right Eating

Proper nutrition depends on what you eat and how you eat. Even when you get enough calories, you may not get the right nutrients. While a lot of nutrition advice is common sense, our society still struggles with it. We are in the middle of a nutritional crisis, with millions of Americans being overweight, even though lots of television programs and magazines are devoted solely to promoting good nutrition. It can be very confusing. Some programs are only selling something, and some nutritional fads are just gimmicks. Be careful, and trust your own common sense. If something sounds too good to be true, it usually is, and before devoting yourself to a certain diet, read up on it and try to differentiate facts from hype.

What follows is my best advice, not only about what to eat but about how to approach eating while in recovery. There is much truth in the old sayings "you are what you eat," and "healthy heart, healthy brain." But as it turns out, our guts also influence our brain, so it's also true to say "healthy gut, healthy brain."

In general, one of the healthiest diets is what's called the Mediterranean diet. Basically, this diet emphasizes fresh food, fruits, and vegetables, and it avoids processed foods as much as possible (which raise bad cholesterol and lower good cholesterol). Essentially, avoid anything your grandmother would not recognize as food.

Lots of books describe the Mediterranean diet in detail. To summarize, this diet emphasizes: cooking with and using predominantly olive oil (especially virgin olive oil), rather than butter or other oils; having vegetables and fruits at every meal; eating lots of seeds and legumes, including beans of all kinds; eating modest amounts of unrefined carbohydrates (whole grains, whole-wheat bread, brown rice rather than white rice); for protein, eating mostly fish like wild salmon and lean meats like chicken; and using milk, eggs, and other dairy products in moderation. Nuts are good for snacks. You can drink three to four small cups of coffee per day and have dessert on occasion.

The recent "discovery" of gut bacteria, our microbiome, is a topic in itself; what and how we eat makes a difference in recovery because our guts do affect our brain by their influence on inflammation and the level of free radicals, which are bad for the brain.

Here is a brief overview of the gut-brain connection showing how our eating habits may affect our brain's health. At birth, our guts are seeded with huge populations and varieties of bacteria, which are determined by delivery and early feeding. This gut microbiome matures as we grow over the next several years. There is no hard-and-fast rule on the profile of this system, and its composition and stability in adulthood continues to be influenced by where and how we live, that is, by our geography, diet, and exercise and by the antibiotics we take.

To help us maintain gut and brain health as well as general well-being, two-way communication — by way of the vagus nerve, hormones, neurotransmitters, and the immuno-inflammatory systems — exists between the brain and the nervous system of our guts. It now appears that some complex neuropsychiatric disorders, like multiple sclerosis, autism, Parkinson's disease, anxiety, and depression, might be related to abnormal gut/brain signaling due to disruption of this microbiome system. Therefore, maintenance of healthy eating habits contributes to a healthy microbiome, which contributes to brain health.

The idea is to strike a balance to maintain a healthy gut, healthy brain, healthy mind, and healthy life. Following the Mediterranean diet can help you avoid what has become known as metabolic syndrome: high blood pressure, high blood sugar, high triglycerides, unbalanced cholesterol (high

LDL and low HDL), and too much fat around your waist. Probiotics, found in fermented foods like yogurt and kimchi, and dietary fiber enhance production of vitamins and antioxidants, and help prevent brain inflammation.

How we eat is also important. Avoid being too hungry, which may trigger craving. The people around the world who live longest and are healthiest are those who eat mostly plants and who make a big deal out of eating. That is, their habits are to make eating an event and to eat at regular, fixed times — as the French do. Avoid eating on the run or eating while doing something else, such as watching TV. Take time to enjoy what you eat — remind yourself that what tastes good is good for you. Drink water before you eat, use small plates — people take smaller servings and eat less when they use smaller plates — serve veggies first, and stop eating before you are completely full. You can't gain weight from food you don't eat.

You can't gain weight from food you don't eat.

Exercise Daily

Exercise is an essential part of good health. Regular exercise keeps you fit and provides structure to your life. There is very good evidence that exercise increases the level of endorphins and other hormones that promote happiness and bonding and that help cut down inflammation and diminish sensations of pain. Research also finds that exercise promotes repair of aging and damaged nerve cells (neuroplasticity) and gives birth to new nerve cells (neurogenesis). So exercise helps your brain grow and stay young, helps your memory, and keeps you from early dementia.

Some good exercises include dancing, swimming, walking, bike riding, and yes, laughing. As much as possible, choose activities that are fun. Get a dog and take it for walks. Walking forty minutes daily, or twenty minutes twice a day, is adequate exercise. It has been shown that even walking a mile a day is sufficient exercise. However, if you can, do more, and do a wider variety of activities. If you sit at your job, get up and walk around every hour for a few minutes. What you do is much less important than doing something consistently every day. Remember, consistency beats intensity, and the best exercise is the one you do.

PAUSE

What are some exercises you can start doing today? When are good times to exercise? Which of your friends might be willing to walk, run, or exercise with you? Write these as commitments in your schedule.

The frustrating thing about exercise is that the people who need it most are often the least likely to engage in it. What these people need is a "kick start." As the old saying goes, "When you give someone a kick in the ass, it hurts, but it also moves him or her forward." A kick in the ass, anyone?

The best exercise is the one you do.

Get a Good Night's Sleep

In addition, exercise helps promote good sleep. We spend about one-third of our lives sleeping, but we seldom pay attention to sleep. We simply assume that when the day is done and we go to bed, sleep will come. Unless, of course, we have trouble getting to sleep, which is common early in recovery. If you have been relying on medication to sleep, consult with your doctor about the medications and about other ways to help you get a good night's rest.

How well we sleep at night depends a great deal on what we do during the day, especially just before we go to bed. Probably the most common reason people can't fall asleep is because of stress. They have a problem they can't resolve or are wrapped up in detrimental thoughts. The next chapter offers some advice for dealing with stress, but quite often the problems we take to bed can't be resolved immediately, anyway. In these cases, a helpful approach is to *decide not to decide*, at least until tomorrow. Knowing that we've temporarily put a problem on hold can alleviate the stress that's keeping us from sleeping.

Here are some suggestions for getting a good night's sleep: Set a time to get up, and get up at the same time each day. Set a time to go to bed that allows for seven to eight hours of sleep, plus twenty minutes to fall asleep. Develop a bedtime routine — some sort of ritual or routine that is comfortable and easy to follow for you personally. For example, check email, deal with any last messages or calls, and turn off your computer before you "wind down" by taking care of personal hygiene, like bathing and brushing your teeth, or doing some light stretching exercise or yoga. If you like watching a TV program or reading a book, do that away from the bedroom — light works against sleep — but don't do it in the kitchen. If you like listening to music as you go to sleep, do it with lights off.

Keep the bedroom quiet, cool, and comfortable. During the day or in general, don't use the bedroom for work or as your office. Avoid bright lights in the bedroom. Maintaining a healthy diet helps with sleep, and don't eat a heavy meal before bedtime. If you are hungry after dinner, eat a light snack. Avoid coffee and alcohol just before you go to bed, and cut down on fluid intake at bedtime.

Avoid Fatigue and Illness

Early in recovery, people commonly feel exhausted and low on energy. Their body is still in a weakened state and is vulnerable to any added stress. Starting a new life to overcome addiction takes a great deal of physical and mental energy, sometimes more than a person has. Be aware of your energy level and rest when you need to. Fatigue can interfere with your ability to function, and it can lead to getting sick, which can set you up for relapse. If you're tired and need to slow down, know that these feelings are temporary and can be overcome with good nutrition, regular exercise, and adequate sleep.

In addition, not everything can be scheduled in recovery. Surprises come up that need to be dealt with. Sometimes you get the flu. When the unexpected arrives, try not to wear yourself out by keeping up with all your scheduled activities. Balance these with rest and coping with illness. Allow yourself "sick time" if you need it, but as soon as you can, restart recovery activities. Most of all, consult with your doctor and your counselor and get help strategizing how to cope, so you don't become overwhelmed. For instance, you may want to keep all your scheduled appointments and support groups but pull back on other activities so you don't exhaust yourself. Exhaustion can trigger relapse, but then again, so can downtime, boredom, and a lack of structure. This is why you want to get back to your regular routine as quickly as possible. Finally, don't overestimate and rely on the power of medications; taking medications can morph into drug abuse. Balance and connection are the key.

Don't Forget to Play and Have Fun

Being in recovery means living responsibly, but constantly having to "stay with it" can be exhausting. It is easy to run out of energy and feel tired or to become depressed or negative. Your new life may feel constricting, or you might find yourself simply going through the motions of day-to-day activities: getting up, going to work, coming home, watching TV, going to bed, getting up again, and so on. Allowing yourself to get to this state lowers your resistance to craving and makes you especially vulnerable to relapse. Drugs can start to seem like a quick and easy way to get relief from being in a "rut," and all the reasons for not using drugs may be quickly forgotten.

At times like this, remember to play and have fun. Find

some new, refreshing activity that provides a break from whatever you're feeling: stressed, impatient, angry, shut down, whatever. The best way to combat boredom and frustration is to take action. Do something. Get physical: Take a walk, play a sport, exercise. Or engage your mind: Listen to music or read a good book. If necessary, go to the library and find an interesting book. Even better, join (or start) a book club — anything social keeps you connected with others, which provides huge health benefits like fighting loneliness and depression. Call a friend and go to a support group meeting or just play catch in the park. Do something unusual or challenging, like learning to play a new musical instrument. Or be ridiculous: Dance and sing when no one's watching. That's exercise; it counts. There's no rule that recovery must be dull and serious.

It's like when your laptop freezes and the error message "This program is not responding" appears. You try everything and nothing works. Eventually, your only choice is to shut off the computer and restart. It works every time.

PAUSE

If you must do things differently for things to turn out differently, consider what you might do differently to improve your physical health. What fun activities have you never tried before? How could exercise be more playful? Make a list and try one the next time you feel stuck in a rut. Remember, it's the doing that counts.

As this advice suggests, our physical health and our emotional health are closely linked. There is a strong body-and-mind connection. Exercise not only improves our physical strength and stamina, but it also benefits us emotionally; it keeps our stress level down and our immune response up, and it helps us think and create. Then again, when we are tired or depressed, sometimes we need to exercise the right attitude to lift ourselves off the couch. Everyone needs to feel healthy in both body and mind, and so we turn next to addressing our mental and emotional health.

CHAPTER FIVE

Emotional Health

~

Sound emotional health is crucial to staying off drugs. How we feel and what we remember are the foundation of our belief system, which determines how we behave and act toward others, as well as how we treat ourselves. We need a healthy emotional brain to lead a healthy life, get along with others, and keep us from relapse.

To achieve sound emotional health, we need to become aware of what we think and feel. We also must take responsibility to change or fix any thoughts and feelings we don't like. Chapter 1 discusses how the brain functions: It describes the separate jobs of our reptilian, limbic, and cortical brains and how these are balanced and relate. This chapter focuses on the task at hand: It deals with the negative emotions that lead to relapse. Addicts often mention certain negative feelings or attitudes as "the reason I used drugs," and when these arise in recovery, they are a red flag. These negative emotions are triggers, and they must be dealt with. How will the addict cope with these feelings: in the old way, by relapsing into drug use, or in a new way, one that doesn't involve drugs? By becoming aware of these feelings, and by learning how to both avoid them and cope with them, the person can avoid becoming overwhelmed with negativity and being swept back to drug use.

In this chapter, we will discuss how to cultivate self-awareness and the mind, how to handle strong emotions in the moment, which negative feelings are the most common triggers (such as anger, loneliness, guilt, and so on), and several strategies for regaining a positive attitude whenever it gets lost.

Cultivating the Mind and Self-Awareness

How well we understand and cultivate our mind determines how successful we are as contributing members of society and how healthy our emotional life is. Successful cultivation of our mind is key to mental health because it helps us manage our negative emotions and the survival-oriented reactions of our reptilian brain.

People have practiced "mindfulness training" throughout human history. Many religious and spiritual traditions promote mindfulness, particularly Eastern religions like Buddhism, and these practices have become almost commonplace today. You don't need to participate in a religion, or be seeking spirituality, to benefit from mindfulness. The core elements of these traditions are actually very similar and simple. They usually include some form of quiet self-reflection, self-awareness, and meditation. Essentially, mindfulness simply means paying attention to our thoughts and feelings, without preoccupation or preconception and without judgment. It means focusing inward to become aware of our senses, our body, our mental state, and our social environment. By doing so, we can give emotions and thoughts, both negative and positive, their proper weight and consider carefully how to act on them.

This is what we mean when we talk about "mind over matter." It could be said that we each have three selves: a physical self, an emotional self, and a thinking self. Each needs to be exercised, so that we strengthen our "brawn-fulness," our "brainfulness," and our "mindfulness." We strengthen our brawnfulness through physical exercise. We strengthen our brainfulness by feeling and thinking. And we strengthen our mindfulness through self-awareness. All three selves need to be balanced, but mindfulness is the most important, since we want it to guide the other two. What we seek is "mind over brain and body matter."

The old masters used meditation as mindfulness training, and

It could be said that we each have three selves: a physical self, an emotional self, and a thinking self. Each needs to be exercised, so that we strengthen our "brawnfulness," our "brainfulness," and our "mindfulness."

as it turns out, they knew something that neuroscientists didn't until just recently. Researchers have discovered that meditation produces neurochemicals that make brain cells live longer and that counteract and reverse the effects on the brain produced by rage and stress. Meditation not only increases self-awareness, but also has positive emotional and physical effects.

While it is beyond the scope of this book to teach meditation, I include below two very common mindfulness meditation practices, a breathing meditation and a walking meditation. I strongly recommend trying them. Successful meditation takes practice — masters devote their whole lives to it, but even beginners can achieve some level of mastery and benefit from the practices. Mind cultivation is always well worth the effort.

Breathing Meditation

Of all the types of mindfulness meditation, the breathing meditation is considered the most fundamental. Beginners usually start with this because breathing is simple. We do it no matter what. However, the ancient masters probably had more than that in mind. In most traditions, there is a very close connection between the breath and the soul — for example, they are the same word in Hebrew. According to the Bible, God breathed his breath into Adam, and Adam became a living soul. In any case, breath is a good place to start.

The focus of breathing meditation is to be mindful of one's breath, but the practice varies somewhat according to different schools and masters. Choose a method or technique that comes naturally to you and stick with it; there is no need to adhere rigidly to one practice or another. This is, in fact, how Buddha instructed his students: They were to reason and experience things for themselves, and each person was to adhere to what made sense and worked for them.

One common method of breathing meditation is sitting meditation. Sit comfortably on the floor, on a cushion, or on a chair; sit cross-legged and straight-backed to make it easy to breathe and to observe your breath. Breathe normally, without forcing it, and observe each breath in and each breath out. Notice your breath from its beginning to its ending; be aware especially of its contact with your nose or upper lip, and of the rising and falling of your chest and your belly or navel. Some masters advise mentally saying "bud" as you breathe in and "dho" as you breathe out. Notice your breath as it varies in depth and rate, but do not try to force it to conform to any pattern; simply observe it.

Usually, at some point, and often at many points, your mind will drift and you will begin to think of all sorts of other things. Whenever you notice this, return your awareness to your breath. Don't get perturbed when this happens; it's the nature of the mind, and it takes time and practice to exercise control over it. By meditating, you are training yourself to be aware of your thoughts and feelings as you observe your breathing in and out. The goal is not to force your mind to stay calm but to fine-tune your sensitivity to its nature, so as to cultivate its agility and its clarity of focus. If your mind wanders, simply acknowledge this and return to focusing on your breath, observing the air moving in and out and all the other sensations that go along with it.

Although sitting is perhaps the most common position for breathing meditation, it can be practiced while standing, walking, or reclining. Begin with a short practice of ten to twenty minutes and work your way up to thirty or sixty minutes. There are no fixed and fast rules; mindfulness practice is a very individual thing. Do what feels comfortable for you.

Walking Meditation

Walking meditation focuses on the sensations in your body as you walk. It is regarded by many masters as the best mindfulness practice, since it simultaneously engages the body and the mind and can thus achieve benefits of both physical exercise and mental training. Walking meditation varies somewhat according to different schools and masters, but its key elements are universal and are what I present here.

Begin by standing straight with your feet comfortably apart, but not too far apart. Rest your arms and hands in a comfortable position: Let them hang at your sides, cross them in front of your chest, or clasp your hands together in front of you or at your back. Try different ways until you find one that is comfortable for you. Next, take a few deep breaths and become aware of your breathing. Slowly return to breathing normally, and shift your focus to the rest of your body and its sensations as you stand. Look ahead, not too high or too low; be indifferent to your surroundings, but do not close your eyes.

Next, focus on the distribution of weight between your feet. Is it equal? Prepare to walk by shifting your weight to one foot. Notice how your body tilts and how your weight is transferred on the sole of your foot, gradually increasing on one foot and decreasing on the other. Closely observe the sensations in your sole, your foot, and your leg. Pay attention to the feeling in your foot before moving your foot forward for the first time. Then step forward and place your foot on the ground. Move forward slowly and notice the sole of your foot touching the ground before you move the rest of your body. Notice how the front portion of your foot bears more and more weight as your body moves forward. Now repeat with the other foot, moving slowly and paying attention to how you walk. Continue until you reach a convenient spot to turn around, then turn slowly around and continue walking in the other direction. If and when your mind wanders, simply notice this and return your focus to observing the way you walk. Do not stop.

Keeping a Journal

Another way to develop self-awareness is to write about your feelings, your thoughts, the events in your life, your plans, and your memories. In other words, you can cultivate your mind by keeping a journal.

Keeping a journal can pay big dividends. For one thing, it's a good way to keep busy. When you find yourself with nothing else to do, open your journal and start writing. Let your mind wander on the page. Rather than fall back into old habits, consider them.

While using drugs, addicts often don't think much about the consequences of their behavior. They tend to act impulsively, based on their feelings. One of the steps in overcoming addiction is learning to recognize and separate your emotions from your thoughts and behaviors, so that you can have more control over how you think and act. Writing is a good tool to help you recognize and understand how you are feeling and why, and it can help keep you from blaming other people and things for the way you feel (see more on this below). Writing helps to clarify your thoughts and to avoid the "emotional buildup" process that frequently leads to relapse.

You do not have to be a good writer to use this tool. Even those who do not like to write or have never written much before find that keeping a journal is beneficial. It's a way to get to know yourself again.

Like meditation, journaling can be done just about anywhere. Ideally, find a private, quiet, and comfortable place and a good time to write when you won't be interrupted. Before starting, take several deep breaths and try to relax. Seek to observe and understand your feelings, not inflame them. If you're not sure how to start, write a response to a question you have asked yourself about your feelings, like, "What am I feeling right now?" or "Why am I so angry?" Or answer a question posed in one of the pauses in this book.

Other productive questions include: "What is going on?" "Is there truly a problem, or am I making it bigger than it is?" "How do I really feel about this?" and "What can I do to solve this?" As you write, forget about spelling and punctuation, and just allow the words to flow.

Finally, consider discussing any issues and emotions that come up during journaling with your physician or in a group session.

PAUSE

If you were to write in your journal right now, how would you begin? Write a few sentences in your head, and if you feel inspired, stop reading and take a few minutes to write. Consider keeping a journal with you all the time, so you can record thoughts whenever they occur.

In the Moment:
Coping with Strong, Sudden Emotions

Meditation and journaling are ideal for calm moments of reflection. However, what do you do in heated moments? Sometimes, strong emotions arise suddenly and we don't know how to handle them. We can get swept up in our emotions and react and behave inappropriately. Or we may deny our emotions entirely; try to suppress an emotion we fear, such as anger; or mislabel our feelings. For example, we may say we are "a little upset" when in fact we are very angry or depressed. All these things can prevent us from understanding and dealing appropriately with our emotions. Moreover, our emotions often manifest themselves through physical symptoms and outward expressions. You might experience a stomachache or a headache when you are nervous, bite your nails when you are stressed, or yell when you are angry. It is important to recognize these outward signs of emotion so they do not continue to build up inside.

On the other hand, physical symptoms can also be the cause of your feelings. You may feel down in the dumps because of a genuine physiological depression, because of the fatigue that persists beyond the immediate withdrawal (known as protracted abstinence syndrome), or simply because you're hungry. Clinical depression may require specific medical management, but sometimes you just need to eat better. In other words, so that we react in appropriate ways, and avoid harming others, we must correctly identify the cause of our emotions while also learning to identify and face our true feelings as they arise.

The problem is that, when strong emotions arise suddenly, we tend to react too quickly. The connections between our emotional brain and our survival brain are fast and autonomous. They usually happen before we've had time to think. This is not surprising since we acquired our survival and emotional brains long before we got our slow-and-deliberate thinking brain. Our emotional-survival brain unit is our first responder to any crisis. Any sudden emotion will cause it to jump into action before we have time to take in the whole picture, which is how we get into trouble. To avoid that, we must practice slowing down in the moment so we can engage our thinking, cortical brain before we act.

We can do this with the following exercise, which I learned from Dr. Rudolph Tanzi, Professor of Neurology at Harvard University Medical School.

STOP and HALT: Understanding Our Vulnerability and Exercising Control

STOP is an acronym that stands for "stop, take a few deep breaths, observe, and proceed."

When you notice a strong physical or emotional reaction, practice these four steps:

1. **Stop** whatever you are doing. Restrain the urge to act immediately on whatever you are feeling. Say to yourself, "Hold on a minute, wait."
2. **Take three deep breaths** to calm yourself down, and smile — I mean really smile. This interrupts the emotion itself and releases the bonding hormone that makes people like you.
3. **Observe** what is going on inside you and around you: What in this situation is affecting you? How are you affecting those around you?
4. **Proceed** with consideration of others. That is, make sure you act in ways that don't hurt or harm others.

When we get upset and "lose control of our emotions," our emotional brain calls on our reptilian brain, its old partner, which is devoted to our survival. If we are upset and feel threatened, this part of our brain kicks in to protect us, usually by urging us to fight (to end the threat) or flee (to escape it). But in many situations, these reactions are over-reactions. They are inappropriate to what's going on and hurtful to others. We think we're protecting ourselves, but we are only making things worse.

By learning to STOP when we feel emotions taking over, we give ourselves time to evaluate what's really going on and act appropriately.

We are most likely to act without thinking, and fail to engage our thinking brain, when we are run-down, exhausted, or feeling bummed out. Counselors use the acronym HALT to remind people in recovery that they are especially vulnerable to relapse in four situations: when they feel hungry, angry, lonely, or tired. These feelings keep us from engaging our thinking brain. When we feel our emotions getting the best of us, we should use STOP to give ourselves a chance to see what is really going on and engage our uniquely human cortical, thinking brain.

By learning to STOP when we feel emotions taking over, we give ourselves time to evaluate what's really going on and act appropriately.

In the same way that our emotional brain is linked to our physical, survival-oriented brain, so our emotional brain is linked to our thinking brain. Yet as I mention above, the connection between our feeling brain and our survival brain has been around much longer. It is powerful and easily activated, and communication is fast and automatic, mostly out of our consciousness. Our thinking brain, which exercises control over our unconscious emotional-survival brain, arrived on the scene much later. It is also powerful, but it needs to be actively engaged. It operates in our consciousness. Our cortical brain is what makes us uniquely human, since it provides control over our largely subconscious emotional and survival brains, but the bad news is that it is slower to respond, and we have to actively engage it to make it work.

The good news is that this effort has big payoffs. By engaging our cortical brain, we can change our thinking, or consider a different point of view, and this helps us change how we feel. Since feelings lead to actions, right thinking leads to right feelings, which lead to right actions.

For example, we may feel sad, mad, or worried, and we believe we can't control or change these feelings. Perhaps we blame others for causing us to feel this way, or we blame ourselves for our weakness. By engaging our thinking brain, we can see that these feelings have nothing to do with weakness and that they aren't being caused by others, and by changing our perspective, we can start to feel different. For instance, perhaps a recovering person says, "All my friends have abandoned me. They never call. I might as well do drugs." By being mindful of HALT and using STOP, the person might change their thinking to: "I feel lonely. Drugs won't fix that. I need to call my friends." Changing our thinking can help to diminish negative feelings and lead to better solutions. In another example, perhaps someone says, "I am so angry she doesn't agree with me that I feel like using drugs." They could revise this to: "It is all right for her to disagree with me. I don't need to be angry, and using drugs won't make it any better."

When we think differently, we act differently, and when we act differently, things turn out differently, usually for the better — and that helps us cope with bad feelings and keeps them from driving us back to using drugs. It is important to realize that we do have control over our emotions. We can change the way we feel by changing the way we think.

You might ask, if we have so much power over how we feel and how we act, how come we still get into so much trouble? The answer is that we don't think as much as we think we do. It takes conscious effort to avoid our automatic survival responses and to engage our thinking brain. That is why we need to keep reminding ourselves of HALT and practicing STOP. That is also why journaling and practicing mindfulness are so helpful, particularly for those in recovery. They create a calm space for our thinking brain to understand what's going on and execute the right command. They slow down our emotions so we can increase our self-awareness. Putting the thinking brain in charge is hard enough under normal circumstances, and it's extraordinarily difficult when we are distracted by the powerful HALT emotions. We just have to keep practicing until we make self-awareness a habit.

> ### PAUSE
>
> *Irving Berlin once wrote a song that goes, "When I am weary and I can't sleep, I count my blessings instead of sheep." How might gratitude help you feel good when you are feeling bad? Do you have a hard time finding things to be grateful for? Consider making a daily practice of expressing gratitude and seeing if it makes a difference.*

Troubling Emotions

Any emotion, taken to extremes, can cause problems and lead to inappropriate actions. However, here are some feelings and emotions that addicts in recovery should watch out for in particular. Learn to cope with these emotional triggers to help you stay off drugs.

Anger

In the early stages of recovery, people can experience extreme irritability, which can result in intense anger or rage. These feelings come from your addicted brain, and they can cause you to lose perspective and rationality, and they may trigger relapse. Whenever you feel anger, remember to use STOP!

Depression

At some deep-seated psychological level, depression is anger turned inward, against ourselves. We feel inadequate and unworthy. When extreme it can lead to thoughts of self-destruction. Seek professional help if this happens or if the feeling of depression persists. At the functional level depression saps our energy and makes it difficult to carry on normal activities. It feels like we don't have all cylinders firing. Depression is common and can be serious, and it is treatable. Do not hesitate to get help.

Fear and Anxiety

Fear is a natural reaction to danger or threat; it is part of our survival mechanism and can, and does, serve a very useful purpose. Anxiety is the sense of apprehension closely related to fear, and the two are often spoken of together. The problem with fear and anxiety is that they lose their survival value when there is no actual threat or they become exaggerated relative to the actual threat. It is important to consider the appropriateness of these feelings and seek help if they are extreme and interfere with life activities. Don't hesitate to tell your doctor about these feelings.

Deprivation

Becoming free from drugs is a very real accomplishment and should inspire feelings of pride. However, some addicts feel as though they have given up all the good things and fun times in life. Feeling deprived turns recovery into a negative state, like something to be endured. This attitude can make you especially vulnerable to relapse. If you feel deprived, use meditation and journaling to think of recovery differently. Count your blessings and what you've gained instead of counting what you've lost.

Loneliness

Addicts in recovery often face loneliness, which can trigger a relapse. They must give up friends and activities associated with their drug-using lifestyle, and yet their nonusing friends and family members may not embrace them immediately. These people may resist getting together with a recovering addict because they have been disappointed too many times before. As a result, addicts may feel friendless and alone. The cure is to get out and make new, non-drug-using connections.

Boredom

During the first period of abstinence and the early stages of recovery, you may not feel much excitement about anything, and you may become bored with life. Some of this flat feeling may be a result of the changes in your body during the recovery process that prevent you from experiencing strong feelings of any kind. Your brain needs time to heal. For a while, life in recovery may simply feel less exciting than life as an addict. A structured, routine life certainly isn't what most addicts experience. Drug users often have many emotional highs and lows, and normal emotions feel flat by comparison.

To put a sense of anticipation and excitement into your life, plan things you can look forward to. The future won't look uninteresting and routine if you don't let it. These activities don't have to be extravagant. Plan to attend a sporting event, visit relatives or non-drug-using friends, go out to eat, take a day off work, or take a short trip out of town. Choose things you really want to do, and space out these events so they don't cause extra stress or exhaustion. Focus on activities you enjoyed before using drugs but perhaps haven't done since, as well as on activities that are personally challenging. What will further your personal growth?

Keep finding new ways to fight boredom because boredom can lead to relapse. Remember, these feelings do change with time; the longer you are drug-free, the less you will feel bored.

PAUSE

Think ahead: What do you want your future to look like? What will it consist of? Next, consider what you can do right now to help make that happen. What activities might you do in the short term on a regular basis? What activities can you look forward to doing over the long term?

Guilt

Guilt is feeling bad about what we have done, and shame (explored below) is feeling bad about who we are. Quite often, guilt arises when we cause hurt in others that needs amending.

In fact, guilt can be a healthy reaction. When we do something that is harmful, or that does not agree with our values or morals, we feel guilty. Guilt is universal, since everyone at some point does something wrong. The important thing is to recognize that you feel guilty, take personal responsibility by making amends, learn from your mistake, and make peace with yourself. What it means to "take personal responsibility" depends on what happened: You might need to apologize to someone for the hurt your words or actions caused. You may need to apologize to yourself for not living up to your standards. Or you may realize that in this case, your feelings of guilt are not warranted or appropriate, since no hurt was caused, or perhaps because what happened wasn't actually your fault. Finally, remember that it is all right to make mistakes. We are allowed to say, "I don't know," "I don't care," or "I don't understand." The important thing is to act responsibly.

Shame

In contrast to guilt, shame is never a healthy emotion, and it often leads to destructive behavior. Feeling ashamed about using drugs or being an addict, or feeling weak or stupid because you could not stop using, is not helpful to your recovery. No one knows why some people can make the decision to stop using drugs and follow through without relapse while others struggle to stay off drugs. Research has shown that many factors play a role in a person's ability to stop using drugs, but there is no evidence that being unable to stop has anything to do with being weak, stupid, or bad. Addiction affects different people differently.

Since shame is a reaction to the person you have become, it must be overcome by a sense of self-worth and self-pride. One of the best ways to foster both is to do something good for someone else: You feel good by doing good. As I've discussed, this is eudemonic happiness, which arises when our goals are unselfish. We do something good in order to bring happiness to someone else. The happiest people are people who make others happy.

Stress

Stress is an emotional state resulting from difficult situations or upsetting events, particularly when those events are ongoing. When you make demands on yourself, or when others make demands on you, that are greater than you feel able to handle, you will probably become stressed. You may, however, be unaware of this emotional state until it produces physical symptoms, such as sleep problems, fatigue, muscle tension, headaches, stomach problems, difficulty concentrating, and feelings of being overwhelmed. Stress can also lead to intense feelings of anger, irritability, and depression.

While you can learn coping mechanisms to deal with certain symptoms, such as managing anger better or improving sleep habits, you must become aware of when stress is the underlying cause and seek to minimize stress as much as possible. There are a number of ways to help minimize the stress in your life. Some of these are simple, but sometimes resolving stress requires major life changes that take effort and time. The goal is to find a day-to-day balance where stress is lessened and doesn't become overwhelming, but no one ever avoids stress entirely.

Try these helpful approaches:

- Invest your time, energy, and money in activities and work that you enjoy.
- Focus on the present; don't let the past or fears about the future cripple you.
- Make time to enjoy music, reading, nature, and personal relationships.
- Tackle personal challenges that increase your self-confidence.
- Break large goals into smaller, more manageable tasks.
- Make your personal environment as peaceful as possible.
- Say "no" when that is how you feel.
- Incorporate meditation or other relaxation techniques into your daily routine.
- Avoid excess sugar and caffeine; these can cause mood swings.

PAUSE

How do you react when you have stress in your life? Do you experience stress differently in different situations? What are some ways you could effectively relieve stress?

Cultivating a Positive Attitude

This chapter has talked a lot about dealing with bad feelings and negative emotions that may lead to relapse. However, you can proactively cultivate a positive attitude that helps in recovery. Three powerful ways are practicing self-acceptance, building self-esteem, and focusing on happy memories.

Accept Yourself as You Are

To overcome an addiction to drugs, you must recognize and understand the power of addiction and accept your personal limitations in relation to it. This acceptance is the first step, though not the only one, to dealing with the problem. Conversely, refusing to accept personal limitations is one of the greatest obstacles to staying drug-free. At best, this refusal results in what is called "white-knuckle sobriety," or devoting every ounce of energy to convincing yourself and others that you have conquered addiction by strictly following rigid rules, which themselves become enslaving. Accept that you have a problem with drugs in the same way as you would accept that you have diabetes, heart disease, or brown hair. It is simply part of who you are, and it will always be that way from now on. Moreover, accepting that you have an addiction does not mean that you cannot gain control of your life. In fact, it's just the opposite. People who completely accept the reality of their addiction do best in their efforts to recover. The only way to win the fight is to acknowledge and accept the fact that you are addicted.

As people in recovery will say, becoming addicted may not have been your fault, but it is still your responsibility to overcome it.

Build Your Self-Esteem

Self-esteem refers to your sense of self-worth or personal value, and it directly affects how you feel about your life. Using drugs contributes to poor self-esteem, though drug effects may temporarily relieve this. In fact, when you first stop using drugs, you may feel a loss of confidence, but that is only temporary. To rebuild your self-esteem, focus on the thoughts and behaviors that increase your confidence. Take pride in being able to stop using drugs, and let this feeling empower you to make other positive lifestyle changes.

PAUSE

In what ways do you hope to feel better about yourself? What are you doing to get there? Besides getting off and staying off drugs, name three or four things that you can put into practice right now to improve your self-esteem.

For your recovery to work, you must learn about the nature of your addiction as well as about the strategies that assist recovery. But the most important thing is to work hard at it. Knowledge alone will not get you there; only action will, which means you must believe in yourself. Virtually everyone who overcomes addiction says that recovery is the hardest thing they have ever done. The truth is that you must take responsibility for your own recovery. No one else can do it for you.

Remember the Happy Times

To be honest, some days in recovery are miserable. And one of the best ways to overcome misery is to remember happy times that are not associated with drugs. Make a list of non-drug-using happy memories and replay them in your mind when you are down. Recalling happy events causes the brain to release chemicals that stimulate happy emotions and strengthen the neuronal connections related to feeling happy. The more you recall the happy times, the stronger the happiness connections become. So next time you feel sad or mad or afraid, concentrate on memories that make you happy. Your brain can only concern itself with one emotion at a time, so let it be a happy emotion.

CHAPTER SIX

Living
Responsibly

~

The lifestyle of an addict requires a great deal of time and energy, and the normal responsibilities of daily living are often ignored. Once recovery begins, however, these forgotten or neglected responsibilities come flooding back. This may feel overwhelming. Just thinking about them may cause anxiety, worry, and frustration. However, taking responsibility for the needs of daily life is another important way to gain control over your life. In essence, you commit to managing your life as part of taking care of yourself.

The first step is the commitment itself. Then you take a reasonable and organized approach to your needs: You make a to-do list, ranking items in order of importance, and dealing with the items one at a time. In this way, step-by-step, you attend to your personal health and security on the road to reaching your biggest goals: connecting with your community, getting along in society, and achieving a meaningful life. Live responsibly, and everything else follows.

First Things First: Taking Care of Business

In chapter 3, I described the eight steps to building a meaningful life. Step 5 is "act responsibly." This applies to everyone, of course, and it applies to all the needs and obligations in life: from work and school to finances and relationships. But for addicts, living responsibly can often be boiled down to the "3 Js" — it's the commitment to stay off junk, out of jail, and on a job.

A responsible life is made up of many actions, but for the recovering addict, the 3 Js are a good place to start. First, you commit to not doing drugs of any kind, but certainly not the drug of abuse. Next, you commit to staying out of trouble with the law. Whether you're doing drugs or not, breaking society's rules isn't a successful way to take care of yourself.

For addicts, living responsibly can often be boiled down to the "3 Js" — it's the commitment to stay off junk, out of jail, and on a job.

If you can do those two things and also stay on a job — or remain in school — then you have, in practical and meaningful ways, taken direct, personal responsibility for your life. These three things are essential for addicts to regain their physical and emotional health and to stay off drugs. Then, once you have a right body and right mind and have committed to taking personal responsibility for your life, it's time to put your house in order.

Getting Organized: The To-Do List

One of the simplest and most effective ways to organize your life is to make a list. Or rather, lots of lists, one for every important aspect of daily life.

For instance, you can start by making a list of the things you need to deal with right now to maintain your life, the "big-ticket items" you need to accomplish. Arrange the list in order of importance, putting at the top of the list the items that need to be tackled first. Keep the list short to avoid becoming overwhelmed.

Next, take one of the top items and break it down into smaller, interim steps. Make a new list that names each action that needs to happen to accomplish the "big-ticket item." For instance, if one is "pay bills," list all the bills that need to be paid, when they are due, and the totals. If one is "get a new job," list the actions this requires: find job listings, call employers, schedule interviews, fill out applications, get references, and so on.

In other words, break each big item into smaller steps. Large goals or complicated tasks are less intimidating and more manageable when broken into easier pieces. Focus on those smaller steps. Do one every day, and before you know it, the big goal will be accomplished.

Make shopping lists for things you need to buy; make budget lists that track each source of income and each expense; make lists of appointments to keep and people to call; make a chore list; and create a "fun list" of things you want to do. Revise your lists as necessary, and add "due dates" to your schedule.

If making lists ever becomes disheartening, stop and take a break; see below for more on dealing with anxiety. However, lists can be satisfying ways to track your progress. Each item you cross off is one more thing you've done to live responsibly and succeed.

Work: Find the Best Job

Once you are past the early stages of recovery — which can require 100 percent of your effort and commitment and take priority over work — it's time to make work a major focus.

If you have been out of work, this obviously affects recovery. It means you have limited resources, and probably too much free time, and you face the problem of needing to find a job. As I say, tackle this problem one step at a time, and make it a priority.

If you are working in a job that you find unsatisfactory and have been thinking about making a change, consider putting this off for six months to a year after starting recovery. Major lifestyle changes are stressful and can interfere with recovery, so wait until you have achieved long-term, stable abstinence. Keep in mind that early in recovery, you are not functioning at your full capacity, and you want to make important life decisions when you are best prepared, not half prepared.

Also, some jobs lend themselves to recovery more than

others. Jobs that place you with people who are using, that involve very long or unpredictable hours, or that pay large sums of money at unpredictable times can make recovery difficult. If necessary, consider changing jobs so that you can work in a more stable environment.

Ultimately, of course, you want work that is personally satisfying and that builds into a sustainable career, though achieving this may mean you need more schooling or training. Don't let this discourage you, but plan for it, and realize that achieving all you want will take time. Work, and building a career, can present significant challenges, but face these issues and deal with them as best you can. Don't be afraid to ask for help from your doctor or counselor and from family and friends.

Managing Money

To truly be in control of your life, you need to be in control of your finances. While money is not all-important in life, it provides for life's basic necessities and a sense of security. Not having enough money is, inevitably, a primary source of anxiety.

When addicts are actively seeking and using drugs, their finances typically reflect their out-of-control lifestyle. When entering treatment, addicts often choose to give control of their money to someone they trust. This is actually a good first step toward controlling your own finances. Once you determine that you can safely handle money again, you should begin working toward financial maturity.

This means a number of things, such as keeping track of

your finances, managing your accounts, and setting financial goals. First, take stock of your current financial circumstances: List expenses, debts, and income, along with the credit cards and accounts you currently have. Is there a gap between what you owe and what you earn? If so, you must develop a savings plan along with a reasonable monthly budget. If you haven't already, open a bank account to help you manage your money. Arrange to pay off large debts through regular payments, and make spending agreements with anyone sharing your finances.

Ultimately, whatever your circumstances, focus on budgeting your money as you are learning to budget your time, and live within your means.

PAUSE

As you consider how to get your finances under control, think about how you have managed money in the past and what you could do better or differently now. In what ways has money, or a lack of it, stressed you out, and what are some ways to minimize that stress?

Coping with Worry and Anxiety

As you take personal responsibility for your life, the requirements and obligations of daily existence may come to seem overwhelming. The number of things you have to take care of only seems to grow, and pretty soon you can get bogged down with anxiety and worries. This is normal. This is what everybody experiences. However, be careful not to let everyday worries build up, since they can lead to relapse.

As discussed in chapter 5, developing a meditation or mindfulness practice and journaling are two ways to cope with everyday anxiety. Mindfulness helps us practice detachment from worry, and writing helps us name and understand our worries.

Another useful technique is to divide your worries into two lists: those things you can fix and can do something about right now and those things that are beyond your control or are fears about the future. Focus on the first list, and take care of those things, and ignore the second list. Don't worry about tomorrow. Tomorrow will take care of itself.

If that sounds impractical or foolish, I suggest that you try this little experiment. Make a list of the top ten, or even twenty, things you are worrying about the most right now. Put the list in an envelope, seal it, and put it in your desk drawer or somewhere that it won't get lost. After three months, make another list of the ten or twenty items you are worried about the most. Now compare the two lists. Chances are good that the two lists will not be the same. Many items on the old list will not appear on the new list, and some new worries will show up. You might say this is to be expected, but that is not the point. Consider those things on the first list that don't appear on the second list: Did you actually go out and fix those problems? I'll wager that you fixed few, if any, of those original worries. So what happened? How is it those worries went away if you didn't do anything about them?

Worry isn't productive; it doesn't work. Our fears are often misplaced, wrong, or irrelevant. If we take care of our lives today, tomorrow will indeed take care of itself, which is another way of saying we can only deal with tomorrow when it comes. If there are problems you can fix right now, fix them and don't worry about them. If there are things you can't fix, why worry? Either you'll learn to cope or life will change and those problems will go away.

PAUSE

Right now, instead of focusing on your worries, consider all the positive things in your life. What do you have to be grateful for? Perhaps make two lists, one of blessings and one of worries, and keep both handy. Every time you count your worries, count your blessings, too. Accentuate the positive; there is real neuroscience behind it.

CHAPTER SEVEN

Personal Relationships

No matter how well they take care of themselves, no one can live alone in this world and live responsibly. We all need to be connected with other people, and in many ways, the whole goal of overcoming addiction is so that you can connect with family and friends and become a valued, trusted member of your community. There are people who love you and care about you, and in turn, there are people you love and want to take care of. Loving relationships foster eudemonic happiness, which increases our sense of connection: When we give love, we receive it, and when we receive it, we want to give it to others.

But for an addict in recovery, this can be difficult. Drugs may have become someone's main, or even only, remaining relationship in the world — whether drugs were "the monkey on my back" or "the love of my life." By quitting drugs, the person has ended that relationship. To stay off drugs, they will have to rebuild their relationships with others. In fact, they may have to relearn what makes a good relationship and how to keep it.

This chapter discusses repairing broken relationships, how to rebuild trust, the importance of developing non-drug-using friends, and avoiding situations that can lead to conflict and negativity.

Repairing Broken Relationships

Nothing in recovery is more important than relationships, and repairing injured or broken relationships is an important step toward a new, healthier lifestyle. Naturally, the place to start is with those who are closest to us, our family and friends.

It is not unusual for a person who is using drugs to hurt other people. During recovery, take time to consider the people you may have hurt while you were using drugs. Focus on this during a meditation or while journaling. Though it may be painful to consider, make a list of people you want to make amends to and why.

Making amends does not have to be a complicated process. Simply acknowledging that you hurt someone because of your drug use will generally go a long way toward repairing lost relationships. Remember, not everyone will readily forgive your behavior, but attempting to make amends will certainly help you begin to forgive yourself. Learning to forgive yourself will then help you to forgive others for any pain they may have caused you, and in time, this effort will help you let go of past resentments.

However, making amends is only the first step to repairing relationships. Next, you need to rebuild trust through honesty, keeping promises, and setting boundaries.

PAUSE

Think about the most important relationships in your life. Who would you consider true non-drug-using friends? What state are those relationships in right now? Are they damaged by past hurtful behavior? How might you improve them?

Building Trust

Repairing relationships is an ongoing process, and success takes time and continued effort. When someone hurts us or repeatedly breaks our trust, we often need more than one example of new behavior before we believe that the person has genuinely changed.

Being Honest

When addicts are using drugs, their activities increasingly become directed solely toward obtaining and using drugs.

This makes it more and more difficult for them to keep up with the demands of daily living. Eventually, addicts find themselves saying and doing whatever they feel is necessary to avoid problems; honesty and truthfulness are no longer considerations.

Yet relationships depend on honesty. Without truthfulness, trust cannot be sustained, and when trust is lost, relationships fail. Learning to be honest with yourself and others is critical to rebuilding trust and regaining lost relationships, as well as for making new ones.

After years of lying and deceit, someone may find it difficult to be honest again. But recovery from addiction is virtually impossible without learning to be truthful. This means complete, not partial, honesty. Unless you learn to be totally honest with yourself and with others, everything you are doing to rebuild relationships will be a waste of time.

What does this mean? It means being honest about how you feel and taking responsibility for those feelings. It means stating things the way you see them and admitting when you don't know something. It means doing what you say you are going to do, and it means not promising what you can't or don't want to do. Being honest won't please people all the time, but honesty shouldn't be unkind, either. By being honest and sincere, you show people that they can count on you and believe in you, no matter what.

PAUSE

How important is truthfulness or honesty to you? For instance, if someone is not truthful in small things, would you expect them to be truthful about big things? In what ways have you hurt others by being dishonest, and how might situations have been different if you had been truthful?

Keeping Promises

Keeping your word is the most important ingredient in building trust. When you keep promises consistently, your words and your deeds become inseparable, and your word becomes your bond. People can count on you because you deliver what you promise. People believe they can trust you, and they do. Keeping promises is a very serious matter. Don't make promises lightly, and never make a promise that you know you can't keep.

For example, if you borrowed something and then lost it, or sold it for drugs, admit that; don't keep promising you'll return it. If you know you can't or wouldn't do something, don't tell someone you will just because that's what they want to hear. Don't shrug off small things or tell someone it doesn't matter — oh, it's just an old TV, you didn't need it. Every promise broken is trust lost; it's betrayal. It hurts.

Keeping promises is much more than simply doing what you've told someone you will do. Keeping a promise is doing what you promise to do whether or not anyone knows about it. Dr. Tony Campolo, a contemporary evangelist, tells a story about his friend, a highly successful and respected dean of a divinity school, who resigned from his post so he could look after his wife, who had developed Alzheimer's disease. His friends tried to dissuade him, pointing out to him that his wife was being superbly taken care of, and in any event she couldn't remember anything and couldn't even recognize him. The dean said to his friends, "You are right, she won't remember what I promised her, but I do." That is keeping a promise.

Setting Boundaries

Building trust doesn't mean saying yes all the time. It's not about pleasing others no matter what or at any cost to yourself. Building trust also depends on wisely saying no when you need to and when it is appropriate.

Part of being honest is setting clear boundaries. At times, it means risking disappointing someone by saying no. But it's better to say no and disappoint someone than to say yes and live to regret it, or not follow through and harm trust.

Addicts are used to making promises and not keeping them; it is their way of life, a bad habit, and they never stop to consider the consequences. In recovery, when facing a difficult situation, it is easy to slip back into this old pattern without thinking. For example, you may have become so used to automatically saying yes whenever drug-using friends invited you to go out that you continue saying yes to every invitation, without stopping to think what it might mean to your recovery. These slips are especially prone to happen early in recovery. That is why slowing down and engaging the thinking brain is so important.

Ultimately saying yes or no has to do with our sense of values. It is perhaps hardest to say no to someone we want to please, but pleasing someone is less important than abiding by our values. Many years ago an evangelist in our church took an interest in real estate investing, and according to him, he had a very good investment deal that he offered to the church elders, which included my mother. My mother did not invest, though many of the other elders, who were her friends, did. As it turned out, the deal wasn't that good, and the church elders lost quite a bit of money. Afterward, my mother's friends wanted to know how she had known not to invest. My mother said she didn't know it was a bad investment; she just felt that a man of God should be minding God's business instead of worrying about his own investments. My mother gave the man some money to support his evangelical work, and he was very appreciative of it, but she refused his investment offer.

There are no hard-and-fast rules in situations like this. My mother faced a complicated situation, and she had to find a way to act that was consistent with her values while avoiding what conflicted with them. This takes judgment and maturity, which come with practice and engaging the thinking brain. It is what growing up is all about.

Making New, Non-Drug-Using Friends

Addicts often isolate themselves while they are using drugs because being around people can be uncomfortable, and this often continues in the early period of recovery. But isolation can trigger craving and thoughts of using.

Rebuilding relationships and reconnecting with old friends (who are not users) is important, but it's equally important to seek out new, non-drug-using friends. Participate in fun, drug-free activities, and go out of your way to introduce yourself to people you don't know. This certainly makes life more interesting, and it's an important part of building a new life. You could also take up a new hobby or take an interesting continuing-education class. Attending recovery support groups is also very important and can be a good place to make new friends.

Remember, rebuilding trust by being truthful and keeping promises can start anywhere, anytime, and with anyone. If you are truthful and keep the promises you make to a stranger, chances are excellent that you will keep your promise to a friend or someone in your family. As you build trust in all your relationships, the chances are also excellent that the strangers you encounter will become your friends.

> *Remember, rebuilding trust by being truthful and keeping promises can start anywhere, anytime, and with anyone.*

Avoiding Negativity and Conflict

As we all know, no relationship is 100 percent conflict-free. But by managing your expectations and emotions, and by anticipating and being prepared for social gatherings and encounters that often cause conflicts, you can minimize trouble.

Managing Expectations

When you start to practice truthfulness, you may surprise some people around you, and they may not react in the ways you expect or want. Indeed, people may disappoint you and make you mad for all sorts of reasons. They may not appreciate the efforts you're making to connect, or they may not reciprocate, or they may even be rude or hurtful. Remember, you have committed to changing for the better, but other people remain who they are, and no one is perfect.

If people don't meet your expectations, don't let feelings of frustration or anger build up inside you. Emotional buildup can snowball and lead to relapse. One red flag is when you start to wage a battle with someone in your head. You think: "Now I'm going to say this, and he's going to say that. Then I'm going to do this, and he's going to do that." Before you know it, you've worked yourself into a tizzy, but you don't really know what the other person is thinking or feeling or going to do.

To illustrate this, consider the story "Wanta Borrow a Jack?" by J. P. McEvoy. It first appeared in *Reader's Digest* in the 1950s, and I read it in junior high school in Singapore. This excerpt captures my point very well:

A fellow was speeding down a country road late at night and Bang! went a tire. He got out and looked and drat it! — he had no jack. He said to himself,

"Well, it's a beautiful night. I'll just walk to the nearest farmhouse and borrow a jack." He saw a light in the distance and said to himself: "Well, I guess I'm in luck, the farmer's up. I'll just go and knock on the door and say I'm in trouble down the road, would you please lend me a jack? And he'll say, 'Why sure, neighbor, help yourself — but bring it back.'"

So he walked on a little further and the light went out but he still could see the house and he said to himself, "Now he's gone to bed and he'll be annoyed because I'm bothering him, so he'll probably want some money for his jack. And I'll say, all right, it isn't very neighborly but I'll give you a quarter. And he'll say, 'Do you think you can come here in the middle of the night and get me out of bed and then offer me a quarter? You can give me a dollar for the loan of it or you can get yourself a jack somewhere else.'"

By this time the fellow had worked himself up to a lather. He turned into the gate and said to himself, "Fine thing. A dollar! All right I'll give you a dollar. But not a cent more! That's human nature for you. A poor devil has an accident down the road in the middle of the night and all he needs is a jack. You probably won't let me have one no matter what I give you. That's the kind of a guy you are—"

Which brought him to the door, and he knocked — not softly, but loudly, angrily. He pounded on it, and the farmer stuck his head out the window above the door and hollered down, "Who's there? What do you want?" The fellow stopped pounding on the door and yelled up at the farmer: "You and your goddam jack! You know what you can do with it!"...

Most of us go through life with chips on our shoulders, bumping into obstacles we could easily bypass, spoiling for a fight and lashing out in blind rages at fancied wrongs and imaginary foes. And we don't even realize what we are doing until someone startles us one day with a vivid word like a lightning flash on a dark night.*

Parties and Holidays

For addicts in recovery, the holiday season can be difficult, and you will likely experience heightened anxiety and stress. In general, circumstances and events during the holidays can increase the risk of relapse. One reason is that holiday parties tend to involve alcohol and sometimes drugs. Parties occur year-round, of course, but they can be hard to avoid during the holidays because of social and family obligations. In addition, crowds of all kinds can be places where drug cues and triggers are likely to be present.

Further, the holidays often mean changes in your normal routine and a loss of structure; you may have to stop

---

* J. P. McEvoy, "Wanta Borrow a Jack?" in *Charlie Would Have Loved This* (New York: Duell, Sloan & Pearce, 1956), 56–58.

your exercise program and miss support group meetings and/or therapy. Then, gift buying and travel are expensive, which may increase stress around money, not to mention having to cope with any conflict or tension in one's family dynamics. It is extremely important to recognize the particular dangers of the holiday season and to take steps to avoid returning to drug use.

PAUSE

Think back to previous holidays. What are some problems or stressful situations you have faced? If these problems arise again, how might you handle them now that you are not using drugs? Before the holidays arrive, plan some coping strategies.

Sex and Recovery

A great deal of sexual activity occurs in the context of using drugs. Both male and female addicts may trade sex for drugs, and risky sexual behaviors are common among drug injectors and stimulant users. HIV/AIDS, hepatitis C, and other sexually transmitted infectious diseases are a serious health threat for drug users and their sexual partners. One way or another, sexual activities are often a significant part of an addict's life.

As such, sex during recovery can be a trigger that can lead to relapse. Often, what makes the difference is how the person approaches or regards sexual behavior. Broadly speaking, sex can be either an intimate or an impulsive act. As an expression of intimacy, sex adds to the affection, love, and connection between two people. On the other hand, impulsive sex is a type of compulsive behavior in which both partners are focused almost exclusively on their own personal pleasure. The other person is virtually irrelevant. Impulsive sex can be used and abused in the same way drugs are used and abused, and this type of sex is not helpful for someone in recovery or for developing a healthy lifestyle. It is possible to become addicted to impulsive sex, which can also be a trigger for relapse to drug use.

In other words, if a romantic relationship becomes sexual, and the relationship is defined by love, honesty, and mutual trust, be happy and treasure this relationship. But approach sex carefully, or avoid it entirely if it is the main reason for a particular relationship. While an intimate sexual relationship may not be perfect, an impulsive sexual relationship is not even healthy.

CHAPTER EIGHT

Being a Member of the Community

~

As addicts in recovery attain physical and mental health and take personal responsibility for their lives, they should steadily turn their attention outward to becoming responsible members of their community. This is the next step toward creating a fulfilling, balanced, satisfying, meaningful life without drugs.

People are meant to live in communities. It is our nature; it is in our genes and in our jeans. Being connected with other people is crucial to our happiness. In essence, a "community" is simply any collection of people who are or feel connected, who help and depend on one another. People who are connected to a larger community are healthier and live longer. Thus, community is the foundation of longevity and happiness.

Empathy and Compassion Create Community

Two important things define happy people: Happy people are those who are connected with other people, and they are those who give to other people. This is no coincidence. These attributes are related, and it's worth reflecting on how giving to others builds the connections and community that make us happy.

In a sense, community begins with empathy, or the ability to imagine what it means to walk in the shoes of another person, to put oneself in another's place and to feel their needs. Life is harder when it's tackled alone, and empathy is how we see that everyone shares common struggles. Others have needs just like us.

Compassion is what prompts us to help fix or fill the needs of others — to be considerate of others, so to speak. Of course, we often help others because those people pledge to help us, too. This is mutual aid, and there is nothing wrong with it. This also builds connections and communities, and it is sometimes called "enlightened self-interest." A group of people promise to help one another, and everyone's life is made easier.

Ultimately, though, the strongest communities are built on altruism or self-sacrifice. The Bible says there is no greater friendship than when someone lays down his life for his friend. While that may sound a little extreme and carried away, it's really not. Thankfully, being a friend usually doesn't require us to lay down our life or, as President Lincoln put it, to give our last measure of devotion. But the spirit of giving, or true compassion, is defined by helping someone with no expectation of a reward. We give when we see a need, and we trust that, in our times of need, others will come to our aid. We treat everyone as part of our community and feel connected to anyone we meet.

PAUSE

What are some of the ways that people have helped you in your life? Think of the big things as well as the little things. Have people only helped when they knew you'd help them back, or have people sometimes behaved altruistically with you?

Don't Seek Friends, Be a Friend

Let's see how this comes together. We want to be happy, so we want to be connected to others in a community. Being connected means having friends, and this requires being a friend, which means giving and being considerate of others, which is the basis of community to begin with.

In other words, if you want friends, don't seek people who are friendly to you. Be a friend first, which will create new friends among the people you meet. People who have lots of friends are people who are good friends to begin with; they are considerate of others and think of the needs and interests of others. This doesn't mean you have to give up your own interests or practice self-denial. It just means being considerate, compassionate, equitable, and fair.

Now, this might sound like a lot of work. It means actively looking for ways to benefit others, with no guarantee they will help you. Besides, you, I, and everyone know that some people are "users." They gladly take with no thought but themselves, and perhaps you have had it up to here with such people. If helping others is what it takes to be happy, perhaps you think it's not worth it, and you don't even want to be happy.

Then again, you don't want to be alone. As an addict in recovery, you need help and companionship to stay off drugs. Sure, some people may let you down, and you may have to disconnect from those people. But if you treat others the way you want to be treated, then no matter what others do, you can feel good about yourself and your actions, which fosters eudemonic happiness. Remember, happy people are also lucky people, and Barbra Streisand had it just about right when she sang, "People who need people are the luckiest people in the world."

If you treat others the way you want to be treated, then no matter what others do, you can feel good about yourself and your actions, which fosters eudemonic happiness.

Being a Good Citizen

We tend to define "our community" as the people who are closest to us: our family, friends, coworkers, and colleagues.

Yet there are many types of communities: the organizations we belong to, the city and country we live in, and even the world, or the greater human community.

Being a "good citizen" means "giving" to those larger communities we are part of. Directly and indirectly, those communities support our lives, and so we "give back" to them, even if the people we are giving back to are largely strangers. We tend to forget how many strangers help us on any given day, but it's good to be reminded.

An excellent illustration of this was a woman who had been coming to our treatment research program at UCLA for a couple of months. One day, she told us she was doing really great, not using street drugs; she was taking care of business and being responsible for herself. I asked her whether she thought she had become a better citizen, and she said, "Absolutely." I was surprised and asked her what made her so sure. She said, "Well, I used to be the biggest pain in the ass for the nearby hospital emergency rooms at UCLA and Cedars-Sinai. I would go to the ER and bother them for hours, refusing to go away until they gave me some drugs. I haven't even gone to the ER once since I came to the program. I think I'm doing pretty good, don't you?"

Well, I had to admit she made a very good point about being a good citizen. She was being considerate of the strangers in her wider community: doctors, nurses, and patients.

In a nutshell, that's all being a good citizen is: being aware of what other people want or need and treating them with consideration and compassion. In daily life, this can be translated in all sorts of ways: avoiding road rage when someone cuts you off; letting the woman with the kid go ahead of you in the grocery store line. Or you can participate in more direct volunteerism: Join a walkathon, donate blood, feed the hungry, volunteer in a homeless shelter. One very satisfying way for recovering addicts to give back is to help other people who are trying to overcome addiction.

There's more, too: Pay your taxes, vote, protest injustice, make your voice heard. And yes, don't clutter up the ER. Don't be a pain. Rather, seek to be a friend and a positive member of your community and of society.

PAUSE

Think of everything you do in your life. Who are some of the people you interact with on a daily basis? How might you make their lives easier, or more pleasant, as you go about yours?

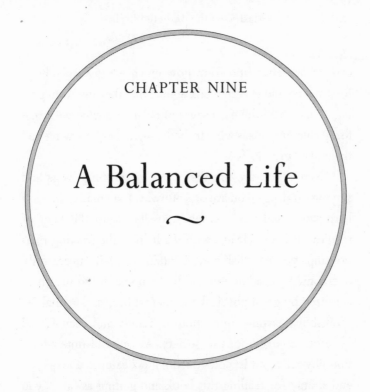

CHAPTER NINE

A Balanced Life

~

A balanced life is the ultimate goal of overcoming addiction and the definitive sign of success. Addiction is a disease of extremes, so achieving a balanced life is a sure step toward overcoming addiction and being successful in recovery.

In the final analysis, success in recovery lies in finding a sense of balance in life without using drugs. We often say we "lose control" with drugs, which is to say we lose our sense of balance and fall, as in "falling off the wagon." Our successful recovery means regaining a sense of proportion. We seek to balance what we take from life with what we give back. We all have certain needs — physical, emotional, and intellectual — and we all have certain strengths and gifts. Our sense of worth arises both from how well we take care of ourselves and from how much we give to others. Recovering addicts often talk about what they get from giving. Thus, in all things, a sense of balance is what we strive for. Achieving this is what truly distinguishes "growing up" from just "growing old."

Even if you are not there yet, by quitting drugs and staying off drugs, you are on your way. Eventually, through hard work and perseverance, possibly with the help of medications, and always with the help of the trusting relationships you establish and maintain, you will successfully overcome your addiction and live a nonaddicted life characterized by good physical and mental health, personal responsibility, strong connections to family and friends, and generous contributions to society. As one old-time addiction physician put it, you go from a tax eater to a taxpayer, and simply for reading this book and getting as far as you have, I want to congratulate you.

However, by this point, you might rightfully be wondering: Is that all there is? Isn't life about more than just balance? Why are we here? What are we here for?

That's what this chapter is about, and as we begin, I have some good news and some bad news.

The Ultimate Goal: The Search for Meaning

The good news is that only by overcoming addiction can you genuinely tackle these questions. Until you free yourself from your addiction, you are in no position to seek the true meaning of being alive, the meaning that gives your life purpose, that clarifies your place in history and your relationship to the universe. Of course, everyone asks these existential questions, but addicts are in no position to answer them. As the old saying goes, "When you are up to your ass in alligators, it is hard to remember that the primary objective is to drain the swamp." Someone in the depth of an addiction is not in any shape to consider the meaning of life; their whole being is wrapped up in looking for the next fix.

What's the bad news? The bad news is that you no longer have drugs as a crutch. You must discover your purpose and what is meaningful to you on your own. But don't let this make you feel anxious or discouraged. Being free of drugs and on your own is both your right and your privilege. You should feel proud to be at this point. The meaning of life is very much an individual matter. It is up to you alone to discover your purpose in being here.

To me, it is logical that this handbook on overcoming addiction ends with a discussion of life's meaning and purpose. The truth is, eventually medicine and philosophy come together, and all the things that matter for a healthy and meaningful life become intertwined. Science, including neuroscience, is an excellent way to investigate the physical, material world, but there is more to life than physics, chemistry, and biology. Some aspects of life do not yield particularly well to scientific investigations, things like good and evil, values and morals, and the meaning of life. Such matters require contemplative investigation.

Indeed, this is where mindfulness, mindfulness training, and mind over matter — or mind over brain and body matter — come in. All of this is made possible by that mysterious sense of self, self-awareness — whether you call it your mind, soul, consciousness, or whatever. The real you is expressed through the harmonious working of the triune brain, and it is far more than the sum of the individual outputs of the three brains. The investigation of the mind has been pursued and mastered by wise people of all ages, and it involves refined attention, concentration, and focused introspection through meditation and other techniques. There is even a newly recognized branch called "contemplative neuroscience" that provides some contemporary scientific understanding of the subject matter.

For instance, one thing we've discovered is that pondering questions about the meaning of life vigorously exercises the brain, and brain exercise creates new connections of neurons and neural circuits — as the saying goes, neurons that fire together grow together. In turn, this increases one's intelligence, intuition, and insight. Even if you don't reach satisfactory answers, asking these questions makes you a brighter and better person, which isn't a bad thing, either.

In any case, the important thing to remember is that our sense of self-awareness is uniquely human, and it allows us to observe our own brain, to have mastery over it, and to exercise and improve it. As with all things, the search for meaning improves with practice, which eventually leads to an even richer and more meaningful life.

To quote the Dalai Lama: "Whether we see ourselves as random biological creatures or as special beings endowed with the dimension of consciousness and moral capacity will make an impact on how we feel about ourselves and treat others."

PAUSE

In what ways has your experience of addiction and recovery influenced your sense of spirituality? How has it changed what you consider most meaningful in life?

What Is Spirituality?

What people find meaningful is diverse and various. Some people believe we live for the glory of God, while others see our purpose as nothing more than passing on our DNA and genes. They believe we are nothing but a vessel, a carrier with no purpose of its own. Most of us lie somewhere in between — we may not be exactly sure why we are here, but we feel it's to do more than procreate. Certainly, when we realize our time on earth is limited, we tend to seek out spirituality. In these moments, as it were, "God" of Moses's burning bush tends to win out over author Matt Ridley's "GOD," the "Gene Organizing Device."

Many people in recovery look to spirituality for the source of meaning in their lives, but even here spirituality means different things to different people. In a broad sense, spirituality means the deepest level from which a human being operates or the philosophical context of a person's life — what defines their values, attitudes, and morals. Others define spirituality as related to our spirit or soul, or as our relationship with God. Whatever spirituality means to you, its role is to provide answers to those eternal questions: Who am I? What am I here for? Who do I have to be to approve of myself? What does success mean to me? What will make me feel satisfied with my life?

To maintain a drug-free life, you must be comfortable with yourself. Spirituality is what gives you the sense of inner peace that makes using drugs unnecessary.

To maintain a drug-free life, you must be comfortable with yourself. Spirituality is what gives you the sense of inner peace that makes using drugs unnecessary.

That said, remember that addiction is a disease of extremes, and it is also possible to go to the extreme of trying too hard to be good or spiritual. Some recovering addicts overcompensate by becoming overly devout, or even addicted to spirituality. As always, balance is the key.

Example of a Balanced Life Philosophy: Buddhism

Many people throughout history and in every culture have been able to achieve peace of mind and great tranquillity by achieving a sense of balance. Buddha is one such example. Buddhism is not a religion; it is a life philosophy, a way of life. While it is beyond the scope of this book to fully describe Buddhism, I recommend exploring what it's about.

Buddhism is a great way to learn how a certain perspective can enlighten you on what life is all about.

In short, the core of Buddhist philosophy involves three basic beliefs: first, that all things are impermanent (*aniccalakkhana*), meaning nothing lasts; second, that all things entail suffering (*dukkha*), or hassles big and small; and third, that all things are nonself (*anatta*), meaning you cannot truly possess anything. Do you detect a familiar ring to all of this? The basic Buddhist life philosophy is not all that mysterious. It reflects what the wise have always proclaimed, namely, that nothing lasts forever, life is full of suffering, and you can't take anything with you.

In the material world we live in, it is hard to forgo all our earthly desires. Some Buddhist practitioners achieve nirvana through meditation and living a simple life, but few of us can do that in the way that they do. Still, these principles are worth reflecting on, so that they might influence the way we live.

Mama Ling's Advice

My mother, Mama Ling, was not a philosopher, and she never went to college, but she was a great observer of human motivation and behavior. She lived to be over one hundred years old, so she had a long time to watch people and see how things turned out. Mama Ling was very fond of sharing her wisdom in the form of aphorisms or old sayings, many of which I now use myself. The things my mother said were not particularly original, but they captured enduring truths, and she used these sayings in just the right way and at just the right moment to wake someone up to what mattered most.

One of my mother's favorite sayings was that the good Lord (Mama Ling was a church elder but not a zealot) arranged the four chambers of your heart into two sides so you can use half for yourself and the other half for everyone else. What she meant was that it is all right to have self-interest and to be self-serving as long as you keep in mind that there are other people around, too, and you should care for them in the same way you care for yourself. That, I believe, was her way of telling us how to live a balanced life. If you have attended Sunday school or church services, you probably know that the Bible expresses the same idea in another simple aphorism: Love your neighbor as yourself.

So, to recap these pearls of wisdom from Buddhism and the Bible: Nothing lasts forever, life is full of hassles, and you can't take anything with you. Love yourself, but give others equal consideration.

That is the wisdom I have to offer in your search for meaning. If you can stay balanced through whatever happens in life, you will do well. Good luck and God bless.

Acknowledgments

I have tried to synthesize what I have learned from my patients over the last five decades into an approach that I hope will be useful in your quest to overcome addiction. Many colleagues have contributed in one way or another to what's in this book, and I thank them for their insight and wisdom. My mentor Jim Klett taught me everything I know about research and systematic thinking. Alan Leshner, more than anyone else, championed addiction being a brain disease. Of my generation, those I worked with closely were Chris Chapleo, Jeanne Obert, Charles O'Keefe, Rick Rawson, David Smith, Frank Vocci, and Don Wesson. Peggy Compton and Steve Shoptaw were my closest collaborators of the coming generation. I am pleased to say that most of us are still actively contributing to this field. The contents of this book — including all errors of commission and omission, goofs, and snafus — are, however, my responsibility. I'll be grateful if you, the reader, will tell your friends what you like about this book and tell me what you don't like.

Finally, I thank my longtime assistants, Sandy Dow and Brian Perrochet, for their untiring editorial assistance; my daughters, Pamela, Michelle, Deborah, and Kimberly, for their encouragement and confidence that the book was worth publishing, especially Michelle, who edited the final manuscript; Michelle's husband, Kevin, who connected me to Georgia, my editor and publisher; and my wife, May, for putting up with me in so many different ways.

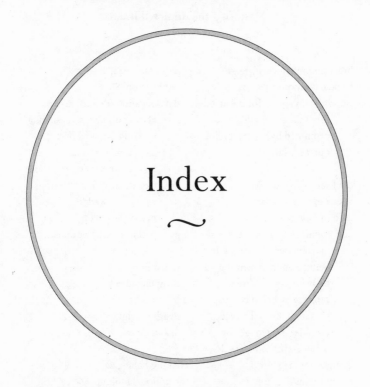

Index

About the Author

~

Board-certified both in neurology and in psychiatry by the American Board of Medical Specialties, Walter Ling, MD, is a neuropsychiatrist in the truest sense. For over five decades he has enjoyed a successful career in research and in clinical practice, consistently listed in the Best Doctors in America, Best Doctors in the West, and Best Doctors in Los Angeles. He has been a leader in developing science-based addiction treatment since the Vietnam War heroin epidemic, when President Richard Nixon established the White House Special Action Office for Drug Abuse Prevention, forerunner of the National Institute on Drug Abuse. His numerous clinical trials through the years have contributed pivotal data to the Food and Drug Administration's approval of all three currently available medications used in medication-assisted treatment — methadone, buprenorphine, and naltrexone.

Acknowledged and respected nationally and internationally as a clinician, researcher, and teacher, Dr. Ling has served as consultant on narcotic affairs to the US Department of State, the World Health Organization, and the United Nation's Office of Drug Control. For the last two decades, he led UCLA's Integrated Substance Abuse Programs, one of the foremost research and training organizations in drug abuse in the United States and worldwide, which has provided extensive drug abuse training to countries in Asia, Southeast Asia, and the Middle East. Dr. Ling is Professor Emeritus of Psychiatry at UCLA, and he lives in Los Angeles.